LENSES ON TEACHING

Developing Perspectives on Classroom Life

Third Edition

LENSES ON TEACHING

Developing Perspectives on Classroom Life

Third Edition

Leigh Chiarelott

Bowling Green State University

Leonard Davidman

California Polytechnic State University
San Luis Obispo

Kevin Ryan

Boston University

Harcourt Brace College Publishers

Fort Worth   Philadelphia   San Diego   New York   Orlando   Austin   San Antonio
Toronto   Montreal   London   Sydney   Tokyo

Publisher:	Earl McPeek
Acquisitions Editor:	Jo-Anne Weaver
Product Manager:	Don Grainger
Project Editor:	Travis Tyre
Art Director:	Sue Hart
Production Manager:	Andrea Johnson
Cover Credit:	Shelly Bartek

ISBN: 0-15-505470-8

Library of Congress Catalog Card Number: 97-74037

Address for orders:
Harcourt Brace & Company
6277 Sea Harbor Drive
Orlando, FL 32887-6777
1-800-782-4479

Address for editorial correspondence:
Harcourt Brace College Publishers
301 Commerce Street, Suite 3700
Fort Worth, TX 76102
1-800-447-9479

Web site address:
http://www.hbcollege.com

Printed in the United States of America

8 9 0 1 2 3 4 5 6   039   9 8 7 6 5 4 3

This book is dedicated to the classroom teachers who inspired us and who will inspire the next generation of teachers.

PREFACE

In recent years, national attention has been focused upon how best to prepare teachers for the twenty-first century. When, how, and where teachers should be educated has been hotly debated in national commissions, teachers' organizations, and teacher education institutions. A common thread through all of the proposals for change has been the need for teacher candidates to observe and participate in schools and classrooms early and often in their preparation programs. However, in many of these early field experiences, quantity has not necessarily been equated with quality. To the untrained eye, one classroom practice could appear as effective as another. *Having* an experience is not, as John Dewey noted, the same as *learning* from an experience. The potential for an experience to be non- or mis-educative is increased anytime the experience is not accompanied by reflection and analysis.

Lenses on Teaching was created with this thought in mind. As a laboratory manual oriented for early, participant-observation field experiences, it is designed to engage teacher candidates in the experiential triad of action, reflection, and analysis from multiple perspectives and through a variety of conceptual lenses. The activities, along with the brief essays, journal entries, and questions for discussion, are structured around different ways for you to absorb and sort out the highly complex situations and behaviors you will be observing. From the introductory chapter, which outlines the rationale for and organizational structure of *Lenses on Teaching*, through Chapter 11, which asks you to outline your perceived strengths and weaknesses as a teacher, this book will engage you in experiences that teacher educators have found to be particularly effective in systematically exploring the teaching profession.

We developed this guidebook to help you perceive and understand the many things that you will see and do in elementary and secondary classrooms over the next few weeks. You and your instructor may find it useful to do all of the activities in the chapters, or you may find it necessary to do only the Core Activity in each chapter. How little or how much you do will be dependent on your background and knowledge, as well as your desire to derive as much benefit as possible from your field experiences. Whichever way you choose to use this book, we trust that the experiences will be educative.

Although the content of this book is ultimately the responsibility of the authors, many persons have contributed in various ways to its successful production. To the many preservice candidates, graduate assistants, and classroom teachers who shared their conceptual lenses with us and inspired our work through their visions of teaching, we are deeply indebted. To the reviewers whose critiques and insightful suggestions made the text more readable and the activities more workable, we are especially grateful. Among the most notable of these reviewers were: Beverly Jensen, San Jose State University; Ted Cyphert, Ohio State University; Julia Roncadori, University of Georgia; Dick Clark, University of Massachusetts; Meryl Englander, University of

Indiana; Michael V. Belok, Arizona State University; John McIntyre, Southern Illinois University; and Lillian Stephens, State University of New York, Old Westbury.

In addition to those who helped inspire and enhance the content of the book, we also wish to thank those who contributed to the production of the original manuscript and the final revised draft that ultimately became *Lenses on Teaching*. The Word Processing Center in the College of Education and Allied Professions at Bowling Green State University was an immensely valuable resource in the timely and efficient production of the original draft. Special thanks go to Judy Maxey and Sherry Haskins for their excellent work on it. Of course, the final draft would not have been possible without the outstanding efforts of the editorial and production staffs at Harcourt Brace College Publishers, namely Jo-Anne Weaver, acquisitions editor; Travis Tyre, project editor; Sue Hart, art director; and Andrea Johnson, production manager. We appreciate their support and expertise in making our vision a reality.

Finally, we are eternally grateful to our families and especially to our wives; Donna Chiarelott, whose exceptional indexing skills were invaluable; Pat Davidman, who contributed both style and substance to the content; and Marilyn Ryan, who served as a constant source of psychological and intellectual inspiration. Without their encouragement and support this project would never have succeeded.

CONTENTS

CONTENTS

Chapter 5   Developing Interviewing Skills   99

LENSES ON TEACHING

Developing Perspectives on Classroom Life

Third Edition

Chapter 1

INTRODUCTION TO *LENSES ON TEACHING*

Many of you are about to embark on a journey back to an environment where you spent a large portion of your childhood and youth. This time, however, you will be asked to look at this environment from a different perspective (or perhaps from multiple perspectives) than you did as a child or youth. You will be looking at schools from these different perspectives to help you in your decision to become a teacher. Although you may have already decided to become a teacher, you may be less certain about where you would like to teach, what grade level or subject matter you would feel most confident working with, what types of learners you would find most challenging and rewarding to teach, what kind of school philosophy best mirrors your philosophy of teaching, and so forth. Part of the purpose of this journey is to enable you to explore these questions fairly early in your teacher preparation program so that you can begin deciding not only to become a teacher, but also to reveal to yourself what kind of teacher you would likely become. Ultimately, you will discover that there is much more to teaching than just standing up in front of a class and delivering lessons.

Over the past decades, research on effective teaching, classroom management, and the role of field experiences in preparing teachers to do both has burgeoned. A recent review of the literature identified nearly twenty-one hundred articles on effective teaching between 1970 and 1987. On the whole, this research supports the existence of effective teaching and classroom management techniques and has placed field experiences in a pivotal position in the attainment of these competencies.

Early in your field observations you will no doubt feel compelled to note useful techniques employed by the teachers you observe. Somewhat unconsciously, you will find yourself drawn to behaviors that seem to quiet down the students, encourage them to work, motivate interesting discussions, and even make students laugh. These "tricks," as they may seem to you, have an almost mystical effect in the hands of an artistic teacher, and there will be a natural tendency to try to mirror those behaviors. Unfortunately, less-than-effective teachers often have "tricks" as well, and these may, at times, seem equally effective in terms of quieting, encouraging, motivating, and creating enjoyment. Differentiating between the deep structure of classroom life and the cosmetic changes through "trickery" will be one of the major challenges facing you as you engage in field experiences. Knowing the important elements in field observation is a sign of developing maturity in the beginning teacher.

1

Holt, Rinehart and Winston

This is the major purpose of this resource manual. You will, in a structured, progressive manner, develop skills and knowledge that will enable you to be an insightful, effective observer of classrooms. You will learn to identify and analyze characteristics of schools, classrooms, and learners. You will identify teacher behaviors, both effective and ineffective, in a systematic, objective manner. You will utilize instruments for observation that will introduce you to a language for describing classrooms. You will discover new ideas about schools and schooling and creating an "ideal" classroom. You will use strategies that will move you beyond objective, fragmented descriptions toward impressionistic, vivid, rich descriptions. All of these activities, through diverse means, will contribute to your development as a teacher.

In order to gain the skills necessary to clearly see what is going on in schools and classrooms, you will complete a number of observational tasks. Each task is related to a key educational area of concern. Embedded in the task are the major objectives to be attained in your field-based observations. Through a series of sequentially organized activities, you will begin to see and understand much more of what is going on around you.

CENTRAL QUESTIONS

This chapter will provide you with an overview of the text to help you understand the recommended activities you will carry out in the field experience component of your teacher education program. With this in mind, we have posed a few central questions that shape the content and form of this resource text. The questions and our responses to them will help you develop a good understanding of the book to enable you to use it more effectively.

QUESTION 1: **WHEN SHOULD STUDENTS ENGAGE IN FIELD OBSERVATIONS?**

In the recent past, there has been a dramatic change in the way that teachers are prepared in the United States. Until the mid-1980s, most undergraduates preparing to be teachers took all of their general education and professional education courses on the campus until their senior year, when they went out to student teach in an elementary or secondary school. There were many problems with that approach. First, most students had to wait for three or four years to discover that, although they liked certain things about education and the teaching career, they were simply not suited for it. Second, their courses tended to be very abstract and remote from the "real" world of children and chalkboards. Third, the teachers in training had only their experience as *students* on which to build. This became very troubling whenever students began teaching in very different kinds of schools than they had experienced.

In recent years, teacher training institutions all over the country have switched to programs that allow for more and earlier observation of schools and communities prior to student teaching. Future teachers are now sent into the field during their preparation. The course for which you are using this text is part of the movement toward introducing earlier field observations that give greater relevance to your training. With this shift in perspective regarding the role of field experiences in teacher preparation, most teacher preparation programs provide opportunities for

Holt, Rinehart and Winston

teacher candidates to participate in meaningful, systematic observations earlier and more effectively than ever before.

QUESTION 2: HOW SHOULD THESE EXPERIENCES BE ORGANIZED TO ENSURE MEANINGFUL OBSERVATIONS?

A sequentially organized and varied set of field experiences should be a key component of this introductory course. The totality of teaching professionals today—educators, administrators, professors—believes that much of the content needed for learning exists *within* schools and *within* classrooms. Initially, you will observe the classroom and school using measurement instruments that will require you simply to record information. These instruments will ask you to pay close attention to classroom behaviors and to track them for short periods of time utilizing specially designed coding systems. These instruments will not ask you to make judgments or to relate your knowledge and experiences about schools and schooling to the observations you make. Later, as you become more familiar with descriptive ways of looking at classrooms, you will be asked to draw more inferences (i.e., make judgments) about what you are observing. As you see more and understand more, you will be creating your "ideal vision" of classroom teaching.

QUESTION 3: BESIDES OBSERVING CLASSROOM BEHAVIORS, WHAT MIGHT BE SOME OTHER VALUABLE SOURCES FROM WHICH TO GATHER INFORMATION?

As you become more adept at participant-observation and more comfortable in your role as a describer of classroom interaction, you'll find that your perspectives are rather limited due to the narrow band of activities that you can observe and record. A technique that is particularly useful in helping you see more with greater depth is *interviewing*. Although interviewing is a more complex and intrusive skill than observing, the range of information made available will be of immeasurable value after you separate useful from inappropriate informants. The *informants* whom you will have the opportunity to interview are students, teachers, administrators, parents, and members of the community served by the school. The potential settings for these valuable interviews include the classroom, teachers' lounge, school cafeteria, playground, school offices, school board meetings, places of business in the community, and, perhaps, even the homes of students or teachers in person or via E-mail. No doubt, you will find these various perspectives on schools, schooling, teachers, and teaching to be sometimes illuminating, though sometimes discouraging.

QUESTION 4: HOW WILL THESE ACTIVITIES IN OBSERVING AND INTERVIEWING BE GUIDED?

Your early activities will have very specific instructional objectives. By the time you successfully complete an activity, you will have attained the intended outcome of the learning experience. Subsequent experiences will be equally well defined, but the outcomes may be oriented more toward problem solving or discovery. One of the major purposes of these activities is to teach you to become increasingly more reliant on your own judgments so that you will begin to see yourself as an effective decision maker.

QUESTION 5:   **HOW MUCH OF THIS UNDERSTANDING OF SCHOOLS AND TEACHING
WILL INVOLVE SELF-ANALYSIS ACTIVITIES?**

Prospective teachers in an introductory, field-based course should engage in self-analysis activities throughout the course in order to discern and describe the changes in their educational assumptions, in the development of their educational philosophy, and in their personal desires and commitments toward teaching. Inasmuch as artistry involves the projection of one's *self* onto or into a medium, artistic teaching is similarly a projection of one's *self* onto or into a classroom or electronic medium such as a home page on the Internet. Artists frequently draw on their past experiences and use their perceptions of these experiences in their art. As a teacher, you will similarly need to envision and clarify your own experiences in learning and teaching for yourself and others to determine how they affect your perceptions of teaching. Teaching style is, by and large, an extension of the teacher's personality—his/her expectations, goals, values, attitudes, dreams, idiosyncrasies, and so forth. In an effort to comprehend your emerging teaching style, you must, out of necessity, come to grips with your *self*. An important objective of teacher education is to recognize that no one suddenly becomes a teacher at the conclusion of four or five years of preparation. You are becoming, and will continue to become, a teacher throughout your teaching career.

QUESTION 6:   **IN WHAT WAYS MIGHT THIS CONTINUOUS GROWTH BE FOSTERED?**

Because of our firm belief in the growth process of teachers, we include a series of activities in the final chapter that are self-education materials designed to expand upon the observation and interviewing techniques you've acquired and to supplement the self-analysis activities in which you've engaged.

This conception of continuous growth and the activities that support it are predicated upon the assertion that American schools have a critical need for effective teachers. Although the much-discussed teacher shortage (especially in math and science) captured national attention in the 1980s, it was reminiscent of a similar problem faced in the 1960s. At that time, the emphasis was unfortunately placed on educating *more* teachers to meet critical needs, and the research concerning effective teaching had not yet progressed to the point that it could inform the burgeoning teacher education programs on the need for continuous growth experiences. Now, as the 1990s draw to a close, we are in a much stronger position to design activities that continually support the professional development of effective teachers.

QUESTION 7:   **WHAT IDEAS AND FACTS ABOUT TEACHING AND LEARNING INFORM
OUR VISION OF "EFFECTIVE TEACHING" AND THE SELECTION OF
MEANINGFUL ACTIVITIES FOR INDIVIDUALS SEEKING TO BECOME
TEACHERS?**

In the past, education professionals have been narrow in their view of learning and teaching. Information was presented, and those who retained it were said to have learned. The range of human behaviors that were considered teaching was similarly limited (lectures and exams on the content of the lectures). So, too, was the conception of learning (the echoing of correct answers).

In recent years, these conceptions have substantially broadened. Now there are many systems or models of teaching, each with specific strengths and limitations. Also, the concept of what constitutes learning has been expanded to include a wide range of intellectual, physical, emotional, social, and technological changes.

Our vision of effective teaching, therefore, has much to do with the kind of knowledge teachers draw upon when they make the day-to-day, minute-by-minute decisions that cumulatively provide the foundation upon which effective teaching is built. In our view, the knowledge shaping these decisions will derive from the individual learners themselves; the culture(s) in which the learning and teaching take place; the body of knowledge about effective teaching in effectively organized schools; and the teacher's knowledge of students, curriculum, pedagogy, and self. From this, several "facts" become pertinent.

To begin with, it is a fact that the act of teaching and learning, particularly as it occurs in organizational settings (such as schools, corporations, etc.), is a *culturally* defined and influenced phenomenon. Schools are human creations like fire departments, symphony orchestras, and professional basketball teams. People put them together in a certain way to do a particular job. Because culture determines so much of how schools are made, future teachers must know not only about themselves, but also about the culture in which they live and work, in order to be insightful and effective. They must be aware of that culture's *subtle* influence on their ways of seeing, feeling, and thinking and must be aware of the culture's *powerful* influence on the schools in which they will most likely teach.

Despite organizational patterns that place one teacher in charge of thirty to forty learners (in our culture) for a day or an hour, teaching and learning are an event, or process, that occurs between *individuals*. Most significantly, these individuals possess learning and teaching styles—patterns of behavior that stem from their individual preferences, needs, and proclivities—that influence the quality of the learning/teaching event. For instance, some students need to see instructions written out, whereas others benefit more from hearing them. These two facts, the "cultural" fact and the "individual" fact, combine to produce a major element in our vision of effective teaching. For us, effective teaching ultimately and inevitably is the kind of teaching that occurs when a teacher's instructional and curricular decisions are informed by the learning style characteristics of students, as well as by an understanding of the cultural, political, and moral dimensions of teaching and learning. Because of the significance and complexity of these factors—culture and learning style—individuals seeking to become teachers in contemporary educational organizations must commit themselves to becoming persistent, vigorous, and proactive learners. Effective teaching is the product of an energetic "learner" who is constantly bringing new knowledge to bear on his or her most recent "teaching style."

But, as indicated, other facts must be considered when one begins to describe a vision of effective teaching. Most prominently, there is a growing body of recommendations and generalizations about good teaching that emanates from the "effective teaching" and "effective school" literature, as well as from the multicultural educational and critical pedagogy literature; that is, literatures which overlap with, but sometimes challenge, the effective teaching literature. The effectiveness literature, moreover, is a double-edged literature. It attempts to define the *reality* of effective teaching by specifying all those things that a teacher will need to be able to do (competencies) before he or she can be certified as an effective, competent, or even hirable teacher. These competencies vary from state to state and region to region, but there is overlap, and our vision of effective teaching incorporates it. We believe that when you see effective teaching occurring in schools across the land, you are observing a teacher who possesses one transcendent skill, namely, the ability to synthesize cultural, technical, scientific, curricular, instructional, and self-knowledge elements to create artistic teaching. The activities described in this resource text will attempt to put you "in touch" with educators who are utilizing this skill.

QUESTION 8:   **WHAT SHOULD YOU KNOW ABOUT SCHOOLING AND EDUCATION IN CONTEMPORARY AMERICA AND THE WORLD BEFORE EMBARKING ON YOUR OBSERVATIONS AND INTERVIEWS IN SELECTED SCHOOLS AND SCHOOL DISTRICTS?**

First, you should realize that your perception of what is happening in school is, in effect, a captive of your past experience. Having spent so much time as a student in classrooms, you will find it very difficult to "see" teaching and learning accurately. If, for example, you were to go far away and observe how an exotic tribe raises its young or, if you were to look back at a nineteenth-century British preparatory school, you would bring to the task fresher, less-tainted "eyes." Realize, then, that you are limited by your own very particular schooling experiences and that this fact will limit your ability to "see" things accurately. Finally, you must recognize that the very reality you perceive, as well as the feelings and thoughts these perceptions produce, are culturally bound and culturally determined. If you were to walk into a counseling session that included a school psychologist, a student, and a parent, and saw the school psychologist performing acupuncture on the student, you would probably be quite surprised. You might not accurately comprehend what was taking place because neither your culture, nor your experience, had prepared you to "see" acupuncture in an American school.

Second, you should realize that schools are a *social invention* that originated relatively recently to solve the social problem of "how to introduce the young into productive adult life." The essential point here is that schools were made by people, and they can be changed by people. As long as the people (taxpayers who fund the schools) are happy, schools will remain the same. When people are unhappy with what happens in schools, things will change if the schools exist in a responsive democracy. As you observe in schools, keep this point in mind and try to discover how teachers and administrators in selected schools attempt to keep the public satisfied and what consequences this has for students.

Third, and related to this issue, is the point that what is taught in school is a community's (not the federal government's or the teachers' union's) wager concerning what it believes its children need to know in order to live well in the twenty-first century. Different communities with different social, ethnic, and economic classes make different wagers. Some communities guess better than others, and as a result, their children are much better prepared to meet the future.

Fourth, schools are complex sociopolitical units in which many of the people and organizations involved are important components. Some of these (teachers, administrators, and janitors) are seen, while some (school boards, banks, publishers, employers, advertisers, state boards of education, key legislators, labor unions such as the National Education Association, and the district superintendent) are often not seen. Each of these units interact to produce the educational reality you see. This interaction also establishes the educational reality teachers feel, that is, the school's morale.

When you collect your observational data, try to appreciate the fact that you are seeing only the surface of a multilayered, multidimensional organizational network. Indeed, it is as if you were trying to learn about the human body by focusing your attention solely on the eyes, ears, legs, arms, skin, nose, and mouth. These surface features are all quite fascinating and do inform you about the human body, but they are not the entire being. As you look into individual classrooms to learn about the role of teachers and of your own possible future in school settings, keep this multidimensional complexity in mind.

Fifth, classrooms and schools are ideas in action. Behind any well-planned instructional activity lies a set of ideas about the nature of human beings, how they learn, what they need to learn, what each child's relationship with others should be, and what worthy ends life can bring. These ideas are not clearly visible on the surface of the classroom, but rather are embedded in what is learned and how the teacher organizes what she or he does. Even if the teacher is not fully conscious of these ideas in action, the ideas nevertheless are having their effect. Because of this, it is appropriate and helpful to conceive of teaching as a moral endeavor (Goodlad et al., 1991).

The preceding questions may trigger other questions in your mind. You may wonder why we believe it is so important for potential teachers to engage in the field activities contained in this text so early in their teacher preparation program.

The answer concerns *attitudes*. Research, as well as our own experiences, suggests that a good number of potential teachers have unusually romantic, even unrealistic notions about teaching in the modern classroom. Thus, for such potential teachers, exposure to other professional educators in their workplace becomes a form of career counseling and provides them with an early chance to examine their assumptions about teaching. There are, in addition, the important research skills of observing and interviewing upon which potential teachers will draw during their student teaching and throughout their careers. Because of the usefulness and importance of these skills, potential teachers should begin refining their observing and interviewing skills as soon as possible.

At this point, you may be ready to ask: "*When* do classroom teachers in general employ these observing and interviewing skills?" The answer is that effective teachers observe their students all of the time in a number of important areas to help make a number of important decisions. They initially observe patterns of verbal and nonverbal behavior, such as in a student's leadership in small and large groups. They analyze interactions between child and other children and between child and adults. They make themselves aware of unusual reading behaviors (such as eye strain), listening behaviors (such as straining to hear), emotional states, physical health, and so on. During this, they learn more about their students by interviewing them, their parents, former teachers, and members of the community.

The emphasis on interviewing may surprise you since interviewing is not typically thought of as a teaching task. In point of fact, however, good teachers tend to be good interviewers. Ted Wheeler, a veteran elementary school teacher in San Luis Obispo, California, now retired, made good use of interviewing for many years. During the first five weeks of school, he would regularly conduct twenty- to thirty-minute interviews with the parents or guardians of each of his students. During the critical "first encounters," he would ask questions like:

Holt, Rinehart and Winston

1. Tell me a little bit about your child.
2. What responsibilities does your child have at home?
3. What do you do if your child doesn't obey the family rules? Does it work?
4. What are some things you'd like your child to learn in our class this year?
5. Do you have any special concerns about the school curriculum?
6. Is your child on any type of medication?
7. Would you be interested in helping out the class (or school) as a volunteer?

This type of first-conference interview will: (a) begin to establish trust between parent(s) and teacher, (b) provide the teacher with up-to-date health and family information (phone number, address, etc.), (c) get more parents involved in public schooling, and (d) set the stage for later three-way conferences with student, parent(s), and teacher. You can also utilize in-depth interviews with students who enter the class later in the year after you have already gone through a good deal of diagnostic activity and with other experienced teachers who can give you additional information and insight.

Another teacher, Paula McGrath of Dedham, Massachusetts, considers herself a "skilled child watcher." When she meets a new class each fall, she makes a special effort to observe how each child behaves in general, as well as how each child behaves in different settings: on the playground, in reading groups, and while working alone. She records what she sees in anecdotal records of each child—records to which she refers in order to think about and analyze problems when they occur.

Ted Wheeler and Paula McGrath are teachers who employ old and new skills to make themselves outstanding teachers. It is our intention to introduce and provide you with opportunities to practice this blend of old and new skills. Unlike teachers who had to develop most of these skills on their own in unstructured situations with little or no feedback about their rates of success, this book will give you considerable guidance. With this support in hand, you should be ready to take your first steps toward developing your skills as a participant observer.

A USER'S GUIDE TO *LENSES ON TEACHING*

We have structured this workbook to make your field experiences as educative as possible. From the central questions we've posed, you've probably concluded that you will develop several new skills, will acquire much useful information, and will realize a variety of emerging and existing attitudes and values. To this end, we have structured each of the chapters in a consistent format that will facilitate your observations and maximize your attainment of the course objectives.

Although the chapters are sequenced in a manner that reflects both the chronology of your field experiences and the intensity to which you will engage in them, you may find it convenient to modify the sequence to match the structure of your unique field experience.

Each chapter has four parts. The first part is a brief essay that will introduce you to the specific phenomena you will observe or discover during that particular visit to the school. The essay will also introduce you to the activities that comprise the "meat" of the chapter. In some cases, the activities (the second part of each chapter) are interspersed within the essay. At other times, they stand on their own. The activities are labeled either Core Activity or Suggested Activity. The Core Activities are central to the field experience and should be completed by everyone, whereas the Suggested Activities can be utilized in part or in their entirety. The Suggested Activities can also be used to augment the accompanying Core Activity, in order to provide enrichment activities for individuals and small groups, or to facilitate the assignment of group tasks in large classes.

The third part of each chapter is the Journal Entry, which asks you to reflect upon the observation you've just made and to record your feelings about the phenomena observed. Your journal entries should consist of your private thoughts, emerging feelings, new insights, and inner struggles regarding teaching as a career. It should be a communication device between you and your instructor, but it may be shared with others, depending upon the course structure. You will find the Journal Entry a useful device for self-exploration.

The fourth part of each chapter is the Questions for Discussion section. These questions involve issues brought up in the essay portion and/or insights you may have gained from the observations and activities completed during that week's field experience. These questions can be responded to orally, in writing, or both, and can also be assigned to specific teams within the class. They provide an important closure activity for that set of observations.

Eventually, this part of your journey toward becoming a teacher will end. We hope that this workbook provides you with considerable guidance as you complete the journey and ultimately understand your reasons for becoming or not becoming a teacher. The lenses that you acquire during this journey will provide you with new ways to look at schools, classrooms, teachers, students, and yourself.

References

Gearing, F., and Hughes, W. (1975). *On observing well: Self-instruction in ethnographic observation for teachers, principals, and supervisors*. Amhurst, N.Y.: Center for Studies of Cultural Transmission, State University of New York at Buffalo.

Goodlad, J. I., Soder, R., and Sirotnick, K. A. (1991). *The moral dimensions of teaching*. San Francisco: Jossey-Bass.

Henry, M. A. (Spring/Summer 1983). The effect of increased exploratory field experiences upon the perceptions and performance of student teachers. *Action in Teacher Education* 5, 66–70.

Jackson, P. (1968). *Life in classrooms*. New York: Holt, Rinehart and Winston.

Popkewitz, T. (1977). Ideology as a problem of teacher education. Paper presented at the annual meeting of the American Educational Research Association, New York.

Spradley, J. P., and McCurdy, D. W., eds. (1972). *The cultural experience: Ethnography in complex society*. Chicago: Science Research Associates.

Chapter 2

ORIENTING YOURSELF TO SCHOOLS

Over the next few weeks you will engage in some intensive observations in local elementary, junior high/middle schools, and/or high schools. These schools may be located in inner-city areas, urban areas, suburban areas, or rural areas. Some schools may remind you very much of your own school experiences, whereas others will be utterly foreign to you. Throughout your observations in these schools, you will be sorting out your own feelings about teachers, students, administrators, schools, and ultimately about your decision to become a teacher. In this chapter we will provide activities that will orient you to the situation you're observing and enable you to derive more meaningful information from subsequent observations.

You may wonder why you are being asked to spend so much time in schools as part of your teacher preparation program. After all, you've already spent over sixteen thousand hours in school before you came to college. If quantity of time in classrooms, in and of itself, were sufficient preparation for career decision making, then these initial observations would be superfluous. Yet, research has consistently shown that early field experiences are essential to both career decision making and to the development of teaching skills in the areas of instruction and classroom management (Lanier and Little, 1987).

Teachers consistently affirm that field experiences were critical to their preparation program, and they frequently bemoan the fact that there weren't more and better experiences prior to their student teaching (Lanier and Little, 1987). What is at issue is how to derive the greatest possible benefit from these field experiences in terms of helping you decide whether to become a teacher, and ultimately in helping you discover the kind of teacher you want to become. By encountering teaching and learning in a variety of contexts and in a wide range of conditions, you will catch glimpses of yourself as a teacher with an emerging teaching style. With the activities in this and subsequent chapters, these glimpses will slowly blend into an overall vision which will become increasingly clear to you as you reflect on your own experiences and on those of others. Eventually you will feel comfortable in characterizing yourself as a teacher and in taking your first steps toward self-direction in your career choice and self-development.

The first step in this orientation process involves actually visiting and spending considerable time in a local school(s). Depending upon your own school experience, your reaction to this proposition will generally range somewhere between thrilling and chilling. Your mind will, no doubt, conjure up images of children hap-

Holt, Rinehart and Winston

pily engaged in activities at workstations, excited buzzing in the hallways, lively discussions in the classroom, and curious learners asking who you are and what you're doing there. You may also visualize faces of kids who are unlike those with whom you went to school, little "rug rats" grabbing you around the leg or throwing up on your shoes, food fights, and the odors that unmistakably tell you that you're "in school."

A myriad of questions runs through your mind—"What should I wear?" "How should I act?" "Will I really be teaching, or will I only be running errands?" "Who should I talk to and about what?" "What will I do with my time?" "Do I have to eat lunch there?" "Will the kids accept me, or will they think I'm a jerk?" Don't feel that you're alone in asking these questions. Everyone feels some trepidation when encountering a new experience, and you're no different. What is different is that although you've been in schools before, you haven't looked at them from the perspective of the teacher. It may take you a while to feel comfortable in that role, and the transition may not be easy. But, the following activities will help you begin.

Suggested Activity 1
ARRIVING AT SCHOOL

Upon your arrival at school, someone in authority should greet you and provide background information on the school itself, the expectations that the school's staff has for you, the kinds of experiences that you might expect to have at the school, and some basic ground rules that will make your stay at the school more pleasant. Generally, the person who greets you will be the building principal or assistant principal, although this task is sometimes turned over to others knowledgeable about the school, such as a guidance counselor or head teacher. To gain the most possible information about the school during this orientation, your group may want to ask some of the questions that follow:

ORIENTATION QUESTIONS

1. How many students attend the school, and what is the approximate average class size?
2. How long are class periods (if a high school or junior high)? How much time do teachers spend on reading, math, science, and social studies (if an elementary school)?
3. Do teachers and students have any free periods (or recess)?
4. What special duties must teachers perform each day or on a regular basis?
5. In your opinion, what makes this school particularly pleasant to work in?
6. Are there special rules or policies that help make the school run smoothly?
7. Are there particular activities or achievements for which the school is well known in the area?
8. Has the school building or the school environment undergone any noteworthy changes or improvements recently?
9. How diverse is the student population? Does that present any special challenges to the staff?

10. Are there any areas or activities that you would especially like us to observe while we're in your school?

After your introduction to the school, you may find that you've formed very strong initial impressions of the school. Based upon the sights, sounds, and smells that you've encountered, you're probably sensing or feeling a "comfort level" upon which you'll be able to operate in this building. What you are experiencing are sensations that are telling you areas that you want to visit, areas that you want to avoid, people whom you want to find out more about, students whom you want to observe more extensively, and so forth. These initial impressions will have a significant impact upon your first few observations and, to some extent, will "frame" that experience by providing a context within which to interpret the experiences you're having.

For that reason, it is important for you to examine your initial impressions of the school and to write them down for closer scrutiny. The process of writing them down will help you to understand the feelings you're having about schools and about teaching. They will also provide a useful point of reference to return to after you've completed *all* of your observations. You may be surprised to discover how your feelings vary from the beginning of your observations to the end.

Suggested Activity 2

INITIAL IMPRESSIONS OF SCHOOL BUILDING

For this activity you should use the following worksheet to record your initial impressions of the school. Many of your statements will resemble a "free association" exercise as you link sensations with impressions. This is an effective way to talk to yourself while you're walking through the building or attending an orientation session. Next, it is important to move from your impressions (based upon sensations) toward a set of conclusions (based upon the impressions). After you complete Part 1 of this activity, try to complete Part 2 as soon afterward as possible.

PART 1: MY INITIAL IMPRESSIONS OF THE SCHOOL

1. _____

2. _____

   _____

3. _____

   _____

4. _____

   _____

5. _____

   _____

6. _____

   _____

7. _____

   _____

8. _____

   _____

9. _____

   _____

10. _____

    _____

PART 2: WHAT DO MY IMPRESSIONS LEAD ME TO CONCLUDE ABOUT THE SCHOOL?

1. Conclusions about the building:

    _____

    _____

2. Conclusions about the administration:

    _____

    _____

3. Conclusions about the teachers:

    _____

    _____

4. Conclusions about the students:

    _____

    _____

5. Conclusions about the community:

    _____

    _____

Now that you have reached some fairly well-formed conclusions about the nature of the school building and how it operates, try to respond to specific questions about the school as though you were being interviewed by someone who had never visited this school before. Be as vivid and descriptive as possible in your responses.

Suggested Activity 3*

DESCRIBING THE SCHOOL

1. Describe the physical characteristics of this school. Is the building old or new? What are the exterior and the grounds like? Does the building appear inviting? How is it decorated inside? Are certain areas carpeted? What impression do you get from these physical facilities?

2. From what you observed, can you tell who is in charge? What incidents have you observed that suggest that some individuals have control over others?

3. How do people dress in this school? Are there differences among the various groups of people?

4. Is there a central or official place where authority resides? What are some things you observed that led to your conclusion?

5. Are some places more physically comfortable than others? Who gets to use them?

6. How are the students working? What are they doing? Are they working individually or in groups? Are they quiet? Or are they talking freely?

7. Are there special areas for public displays? If so, what is in them, and what do they say about this school? Go into the teachers' lounge(s) and places where teachers eat and observe the physical facilities, the information on the bulletin boards, the behavior of individuals, and if and how that behavior differs from "public" behavior. What are some of the topics people talk about?

8. Finally, report anything that happened to you in the process of making the observation. This includes encounters with people or questions about what you were doing. Also, comment on things that you expected to happen that did not. Conclude by giving your general impressions of the school you visited.

*(Ryan, Burkholder, and Phillips, 1983)

Holt, Rinehart and Winston

Are the classrooms you are observing organized to enhance student learning?

"And then, of course, there's the possibility of being just the slightest bit too organized."

Glen Dines KAPPAN
Holt, Rinehart and Winston

Although school buildings have a considerable amount of commonality, classrooms are quite diverse in the way that they are arranged, decorated, and used. Classrooms appear to have a personality, and that personality is a curious blend of the teacher's style and the students' needs and values. Classrooms offer interesting contrasts in both form and function. Some classrooms appear to be living spaces, whereas others appear to be work places. Some are vividly decorated and vibrant in tone, whereas others are stark and uninviting. Although elementary classrooms seem to be more inviting than secondary classrooms, some secondary classrooms excite both the senses and the imagination. However, because secondary teachers often move from room to room in their day's teaching, the cumulative effect is to have secondary classrooms lacking the fine touches that often accumulate in delightful ways in elementary classrooms.

Because the bulk of your observation time will be spent in the classroom, there should be ample opportunity to sketch out a detailed map that depicts where the teacher and students are located as well as unique features of the room's organization. Besides showing the physical layout of the classroom, identify the more subtle features as well. For example, is the room lighted naturally or artificially? Are desks designed for maximum mobility? Does the physical arrangement of the desks facilitate the use of a variety of teaching strategies? Are bulletin boards or displays coordinated with the unit or course content? Is media hardware (i.e., televisions, computers, overhead projectors, screens) located in such a way as to enhance instruction and learning (Emmer, Evertson, Stanford, Clements, and Worsham, 1983)?

Next is an "aerial" view of an empty classroom. Use this space to illustrate the classroom you're observing. Include as much detail as possible.

Core Activity

MAPPING THE CLASSROOM

Student Name: _____ Date: _____

Based on your map, respond to the following questions:

1. In what ways is the organization of the classroom conducive to student learning? In what ways does it inhibit learning?

2. Given this classroom organization, what would you expect to be important elements of the teacher's philosophy or style of teaching?

3. Do the students and the teacher appear to be comfortable with the classroom organization? On what do you base this conclusion?

4. If you were the teacher, how would you modify this classroom to fit your style of teaching?

During this first visit to the school, you've encountered many individuals who made an impression upon you. These individuals may have included an administrator who introduced you to the school building and to your cooperating teacher, the classroom teacher whom you observed, or a student (or students) to whom you were drawn throughout the observation. Or these individuals could have been even a person on the school staff such as the office secretary, a maintenance worker, or a cafeteria helper. Over the next few weeks these individuals may have a considerable impact on your decision to become a teacher, and it will be useful to think about how these people might affect your perceptions of schools, teaching, and learning.

Based upon this initial contact, try to identify *the* person who made the *most vivid* impression on you and analyze why he or she affected you this way. The impression may have been either positive or negative, but the critical element will be to discern how this individual might alter or enhance your perceptions of a career in teaching. Use the form that follows to describe, analyze, and evaluate the impression this individual made upon you.

Suggested Activity 4

THE MOST MEMORABLE PERSON

1. Description of the Person Who Made the Most Vivid Impression Upon Me (include in this description the role that this person had in the school, how you interacted with him/her, and a brief discussion of what he/she did to make such a vivid impression on you):

2. Analysis of Why This Person Might Affect My Perceptions of the School (include in this analysis a description of how this person affected you, in what way he/she altered your perceptions, and why he/she might influence your decision about teaching):

3. Evaluation of the Person Who Impressed Me Most Vividly (include in this evaluation your feelings about why this person might influence you, what you've discovered about yourself through interacting with this person, and whether you should allow your perceptions to be influenced by him/her):

Your first observation in the school has left you with a variety of feelings, some vivid impressions, and a tremendous number of questions. Use these feelings, impressions, and questions to generate a list of things that you would like to do or see in your remaining observations. The Journal Entry that follows is a logical place to include this list as well as to record a few of your reactions. Because this is your first Journal Entry, you should complete it as soon as possible after your visit to the school.

Holt, Rinehart and Winston

Student Name: _____   Date: _____

Journal Entry

Because this is your first Journal Entry of your first impressions of the school and of the teacher(s) whom you are observing, use those impressions as the focal point of this entry. Concentrate on the school structure, its functional nature, and its aesthetic qualities. How do you feel about the school and the conditions under which teaching and learning occur? What are your initial impressions of the teacher's workload? How would you summarize your feelings about teaching right now?

_____

_____

_____

_____

_____

_____

_____

_____

_____

_____

_____

_____

_____

_____

_____

_____

_____

_____

_____

_____

Questions for Discussion

1. Based on your initial observations, what are your impressions of the school and its role in the education of the community? What are your impressions of the teacher and his/her role(s) in the school? Did those impressions change from what they were before your observation? Why?

2. Critically analyze your impressions of the school. What aspects of the school made the biggest impression on you? Were most of your impressions positive or negative? How might these impressions affect later observations?

3. Critically analyze the classroom that you observed in terms of its physical arrangement. In what ways is the physical arrangement conducive to teaching and learning? In what ways is it detrimental? If this were your classroom, how would you change it?

4. Describe your feelings as you took your walking tour of the school. What impressed you regarding its physical structure, organization, resources, aesthetics, and so forth? What did you dislike about it? Did you regard the school as inviting or discouraging learning? In what ways might your impressions change during subsequent observations?

References

Emmer, E. T., Evertson, C. M., Sanford, J. P., Clements, B. S., and Worsham, M. E. (1983). *Organizing and managing the junior high school classroom* (pp. 6–15). Austin: The Research and Development Center for Teacher Education (University of Texas at Austin).

Lanier, J., and Little, J. (1987). Research on teacher education. In *Handbook of research on teaching* (3rd ed.), edited by Merlin C. Wittrock (pp. 550–552). New York: Macmillan.

Ryan, K., Burkholder, S., and Phillips, D. H. (1983). *The workbook: Exploring careers in teaching* (pp. 49–50). Columbus, Ohio: Merrill.

Holt, Rinehart and Winston

Chapter 3

SCHOOL RESTRUCTURING AND TEACHERS' PROFESSIONAL DEVELOPMENT

During your first observation(s) you collected some strong impressions of the school building, its classrooms, a teacher's workday, and, to some extent, the role of the administrator. Chances are you synthesized these impressions with little effort and concluded whether or not your assigned school was using "best practices." You based this conclusion largely on how *you* would like a school to operate and on how closely this school's operation matched your ideal of say, the elementary or high school you attended. If this school's operation closely mirrored your own school's, it must be using "best practices." These conclusions are generally useful because they help frame our experiences and provide guidance as to the kind of school settings in which we'd feel comfortable working.

Conclusions, however, are useful only to the extent that the evidence upon which they're based is solid. Initial impressions, though powerful, can be misleading. In this chapter, you will be given structured activities that will help you collect evidence on innovative practices that may be occurring in the school(s) you are observing. This evidence may support or refute your initial impressions, but it will definitely strengthen the evidence upon which you base your conclusions.

RESTRUCTURED SCHOOLS

In the late 1980s educators began to write about and to create schools that represented best practices. These schools were labeled "restructured schools," and they bore many of the characteristics associated with such prescriptive practices as site-based management, teacher empowerment, total quality management, cooperative learning, integrated curricula, authentic assessment, cross-age grouping, and so forth. The restructured schools represented another kind of effectiveness—predicated on the assumption that effectiveness is synonymous with shared decision making and collaboration rather than with higher test scores and mastery of basic skills.

Although there is no "one best model" of restructured schools, attempts have been made by research centers such as the National Center on Organization and Restructuring of Schools (NCORS) to develop categories for identifying schools that are implementing the strategies just discussed (cited in Griswold, 1992). The range of

Holt, Rinehart and Winston

possibilities for restructuring is quite wide and includes such minimal changes as providing cross-disciplinary teams of teachers and such extensive changes as flexible scheduling, schools within a school, year-round calendars, and so forth. Indeed, a number of model school designs have been incorporated into the restructuring movement, thus apparently providing an "umbrella" label for such time-honored practices as individually guided education, mastery learning, modular scheduling, cross-age grouping, and so forth. Although the term *restructuring* is a recent manifestation, it is clear that some of the recommended changes have been in existence since the heyday of progressive education.

Restructuring has focused attention on a fundamental societal shift that has occurred in the past twenty-five years, a shift of which schools are now only beginning to become aware. When agrarian and industrial structures dominated the major institutions of society (i.e., churches, schools, businesses, the family), the linear, segmented, bureaucratic, specialized manner in which people organized their lives made considerable sense. Since the electronic revolution of the post–World War II era, however, society has begun to shift more and more away from an Industrial/Agricultural Age mentality to an Information Age mentality. To survive, institutions must shift when society shifts. Those traditional industrially/agriculturally based structure of schools made sense in the early 1900s. Today such schools are anachronisms.

The advocates of restructuring suggest that schools must begin to adopt models that reflect the Information Age and not the Industrial/Agricultural Age. Ideally, because vestiges of the industrial/agricultural model still exist in society, and more importantly in people's minds, schools will need to maintain aspects of both models. However, Information Age models will begin to be the dominant force in the coming century.

Practically speaking, schools will begin to incorporate new structures for administration (e.g., total quality management that stresses participatory decision making rather than hierarchical, authoritarian relationships), for curriculum (e.g., integrated, cross-disciplinary approaches that stress the interrelationship of content rather than arbitrary subject-matter distinctions), for methodology (e.g., cooperative, cross-age grouping of learners with a focus on interdisciplinary projects rather than individual deskwork), and for learning (e.g., emphasizing mastery of content rather than coverage of content and constructivist rather than behaviorist thinking strategies). As a result of these changes, school buildings themselves will begin to take on a different look. There will be fewer individual classrooms monitored by a single teacher. Class "periods" will no longer be established for a fixed time frame. Textbooks and other instructional resources will become part of a database rather than the main feature of the curriculum. Students will be grouped developmentally rather than chronologically, and cultural diversity will become the rule rather than the exception. In short, both the structure and the function of schools will change, and restructuring, now an ideal, will become a reality.

The following Suggested Activity asks you to create a new school structure more in keeping with changes created by the Information Age. To facilitate this activity, you are given two columns, one representing school structures in the Industrial Age and the other representing school structures in the Information Age. Describe what currently exists in the schools that you attended and/or are observing and then describe the changes needed to attain the goals of restructuring. You may want to complete Column A as a whole class or in a group activity and then complete Column B on your own.

Suggested Activity 1

RESTRUCTURED SCHOOLS

Student Name: _____   Date: _____

In this activity, describe an elementary, middle school, high school, or K–12 school that utilizes an Industrial Age structure. Then, restructure that school to fit the changes caused by the shift to an Information Age structure.

A
INDUSTRIAL AGE SCHOOL
school design

B
INFORMATION AGE SCHOOL
school design

school calendar

school calendar

school schedule

school schedule

classroom design

classroom design

student grouping   student grouping

curriculum organization   curriculum organization

teacher's role   teacher's role

classroom activities   classroom activities

school administration   school administration

role (image) of the learner   role (image) of the learner

SCHOOL IMPROVEMENT MODELS[1]

As part of the Goals 2000 initiatives, the federal government began allocating monies to each state to stimulate more local school reform and restructuring efforts. These monies were intended to increase collaboration between and among such disparate groups as pre K–12 educators, school administrators, college faculty, parents, students, and business and industry. The stated purpose was to increase everyone's stake in improving the quality of education at the state level and ultimately nationally. The assumption was that grass roots effort would yield more involvement and hence more meaningful, long-term change.

As schools began to vie for these monies to stimulate change, models for school improvement began to emerge both in the literature and in practice. Some of these models emerged from single individuals working with individual schools or school systems, whereas others emerged as national projects or through changing standards by which schools were accredited. By 1996 enough different models had emerged that the Ohio Department of Education was able to provide a summary of nine models that pre K–12 schools could adopt or adapt in their local efforts at school restructuring and reform. The following section describes the nine models as summarized by the Ohio Department of Education, but these descriptions are consistent with those used by other states as they sought to provide guidance for change in their local schools. As you read through these models, you may find it useful to note specific indicators that earmark each model. Then, apply these indicators to the school in which you are observing. Is your school utilizing one of these models or aspects of one or more of these models, or is it creating a model unique to that school? Or, are you unable to identify any indicators of the school improvement models in the school that you are observing? In that case, which model would you recommend for that school?

ACCELERATED SCHOOLS (LEVIN)

Since the mid-1980s more than three hundred elementary schools across the country have initiated the Accelerated Schools model, a comprehensive approach to school change designed by Henry M. Levin and colleagues at Stanford University to enable *all* students to enter secondary school in the educational mainstream. The Accelerated Schools project is both a way of thinking about academic acceleration for all students and a concrete process for achieving it. The philosophy centers around creating the kind of schools for *all* children—"dream schools"—that we would want our own children to attend.

The Accelerated Schools model targets students who are educationally at-risk because they begin school with learning gaps in areas valued by schools and mainstream economic and social institutions. Instead of slowing down instruction for lower-ability students, Accelerated Schools speed up instruction to help these students catch up with their peers. Accelerated Schools display the following characteristics: high expectations on the part of teachers, parents, and students; deadlines by

---

[1]Taken from guidelines issued by the Ohio Department of Education (1996).

which students are expected to meet particular educational requirements; stimulating and relevant instructional programs; and involvement of the teachers, parents, and the community in the design and implementation of programs. The Accelerated Schools approach also creates a strong sense of self-worth and educational accomplishments for students.

The Accelerated Schools model has three guiding principles:

1. *Unity of purpose:* Passion and commitments, not formal mission statements, create the strong school structure with students at the top.
2. *Empowerment coupled with responsibility:* Decisions are made at the school site regarding resources, personnel, curriculum, and assessment.
3. *Building on strengths* (of teaching and learning): Students' performance is assessed not only on standardized tests and formal assessments, but also on other measures.

In addition, a fundamental set of values underlying these principles is necessary to establish integrated curricular, instructional, and organizational changes. The entire curriculum should be enriched and emphasize language development in all subjects. Instructional practices should promote active learning experiences through the use of cross-age tutoring and cooperative learning. The organization of an Accelerated School should be characterized by broad participation in decision making by administrators, teachers, and parents.

SCHOOL DEVELOPMENT PROGRAM (COMER)

The School Development Program (SDP) was developed by 1986 by renowned child psychiatrist Dr. James Comer as a collaborative effort between the Yale University Child Study Center and the New Haven School District. The SDP, or Comer Process, brings together parents, teachers, and mental-health workers to create a positive social climate in schools that serve poor and minority children. Comer schools improve students' academic performance by addressing the underlying social and psychological issues that interfere with learning. Adults in children's lives—at home, at school, and in the community—are asked to join together to support and to nurture each child's total development so that each can reach his or her full potential.

The SDP is a nine-component systemic change model consisting of three mechanisms, three operations, and three guidelines. Fostering positive parent-school relationships is an essential ingredient of the Comer model. It calls for three fundamental mechanisms:

1. A governance and management team representing parents, teachers, administrators, and support staff
2. A mental-health or support staff team to address individual behavior problems and to consider how school practices can be changed to prevent problems
3. A parent program to increase parental involvement

The governance and management team carries out three critical operations: the development of (4) a comprehensive school plan with specific goals in the social climate and academic areas, (5) staff/development activities based on building-level goals in these areas, and (6) periodic assessment that allows the staff to adjust the program to meet identified needs and opportunities.

Holt, Rinehart and Winston

Several important guidelines and agreements are needed. Participants on the governance and management team (7) cannot paralyze the leader. On the other hand, the leader cannot use the team as a "rubber stamp." Although the principal usually provides leadership to the governance and management team, (8) decisions are made by consensus to avoid "winner-loser" feelings and behavior. And (9) a "no-fault" problem-solving approach is used by all of the working groups in the school, and eventually these attitudes permeate the thinking of most individuals.

The SDP is not a quick fix or an easy solution. The governance and management team plays a vital role in giving the school a sense of direction, providing communication, and, most importantly, allowing everyone to experience a sense of ownership in the outcome of the program. When carried out by reasonably motivated and competent people the Comer model can produce improved academic and social achievement of students and an improved school operation.

COALITION OF ESSENTIAL SCHOOLS (SIZER)

The Coalition of Essential Schools was established in 1984 by Theodore R. Sizer, a professor at Brown University, as a high school–university partnership designed to strengthen the learning of students by reforming school priorities and simplifying school structures. Each Essential School applies a core of nine common principles in order to develop its own unique plan. These nine common principles are:

1. The school should focus on helping adolescents learn to use their minds well. A school should not attempt to be "comprehensive" if such a claim is made at the expense of the school's central intellectual purpose.

2. The school's goals should be simple: that each student master a limited number of essential skills and areas of knowledge. Curricular decisions should be based on thorough student mastery and achievement rather than on an effort merely to cover (subject) content areas.

3. The school's goals should apply to all students, whereas the means to these goals should vary depending on the student. School practice should be customized to meet the needs of every group or class of adolescents.

4. Teaching and learning should be personalized to the maximum feasible extent. Decisions about the course of study, the use of time, and the choice of teaching materials and specific pedagogies must be placed into the hands of the principal and staff.

5. The governing practical metaphor of the school should be student-as-worker. A prominent pedagogy will be coaching, to provoke students to learn and thus to teach themselves.

6. For graduation, students should be awarded a diploma upon successful final demonstration of mastery—an "exhibition." There is no strict age grading and no system of "credits earned" by "time spent" in class. The emphasis is on the student's demonstration that he or she can do important things.

7. The tone of the school should stress the values of unanxious expectation ("I won't threaten you, but I expect much of you"), of trust (until abused), and of decency (the values of fairness, generosity, and tolerance).

8. The principal and teachers should perceive themselves as generalists first and specialists second.

9. Administrative/budget targets should be: eighty or fewer students per teacher, substantial time for collective planning by teachers, competitive salaries for staff, and an ultimate per-student cost not to exceed that in traditional schools by more than 10 percent.

EFFECTIVE SCHOOLS

The Effective Schools Process (ESP) is a comprehensive, collegial site-based management process to improve students' academic achievement. The Effective Schools Process affects all students regardless of abilities, cuts across all curriculum areas, and examines all areas that affect academic achievement. Everyone is involved: administrators, teachers, support staff, parents, students, and business and community leaders.

The ESP is built upon four assumptions: All children can learn; increased academic achievement is the mark of effectiveness; leadership must be building-based;

Based on your observations, is the principal a strong, positive influence on the school?

"We don't have a leader here, just our principal, Mr. Langburn."

Originally published in Phi Delta Kappan
Holt, Rinehart and Winston

and school improvement plans must be tailored to the needs of the students, teachers, and administrators.

There are seven factors of Effective Schools:

1. *A sense of mission.* Each school makes a conscious decision to become an Effective School. A collegial decision and commitment are made to assure minimum mastery of basic school skills for all students.
2. *Strong building leadership.* The principals are, in fact, the instructional leaders of the staff. They are creative, bold, supportive, and dedicated to the mission of the school. They are active and involved with all parts of the education community.
3. *High expectations for all students and staff.* Effective Schools expect teachers to teach and students to learn. Standards are high but realistic. No student is allowed to attain less than minimum mastery of the basic skills of the assigned level.
4. *Frequent monitoring of student progress.* Teachers and principals are constantly aware of and monitor student progress in relation to the instructional objectives.
5. *A positive learning climate.* The climate is warm and responsive, emphasizes cognitive development, is innovative, and provides a student support system.
6. *Sufficient opportunity for learning.* Effective Schools emphasize more time on task to increase learning. This implies improved use of time, more individualized instruction, and sufficient curricular content.
7. *Parent/community involvement.* Effective Schools have broad support from parents and the larger education community.

The Ohio Building Leadership model provides the direction for how to implement the ESP. This model includes forming the principal-led team, developing and conducting a needs assessment, sharing the needs assessment with the total staff, developing and implementing the action plan, and providing ongoing assessment and evaluation.

SUCCESS FOR ALL SCHOOLS (SLAVIN)

At the current time, many at-risk children are allowed to fall behind until they are labeled in some way—*learning disabled, economically disadvantaged,* or *emotionally disturbed*—and are then provided remedial instruction that rarely succeeds in raising them to the level of their classmates. Success for All believes that school failure, especially reading failure, can be prevented with virtually all students, regardless of background.

Success for All is a schoolwide program for students in grades pre K–5 that reorganizes school and community resources to ensure that virtually every student will make it through the third grade at or near grade level in reading and other basic skills and that then goes beyond this performance level in the later grades. The goal of Success for All is to prevent academic deficits from appearing in the first place, to recognize and intensively intervene when any deficits do appear, and to provide at-risk students with a rich and full curriculum to enable them to build on their firm foundation in basic skills.

Developed in 1986 by Robert Slavin (codirector) and the staff of the Center for Research on Effective Schooling for Disadvantaged Students at Johns Hopkins University in Baltimore, Success for All has the following basic elements:

1. *Tutors.* In grades one to three, specially trained certified teachers work one-to-one with students who are struggling to keep up with their classmates in reading. Daily twenty-minute tutoring classes are closely connected with classroom instruction.

2. *Schoolwide curriculum.* During reading periods, students are regrouped across age lines so that each reading class contains students at only one reading level. The program emphasizes cooperative learning activities, a combination of phonetic teaching and whole language, and a wide variety of modalities to teach reading success.

3. *Preschool and kindergarten.* The program emphasizes language development, readiness, and self-concept.

4. *Eight-week assessments.* Students in grades K–3 are assessed every eight weeks to determine whether they are making adequate progress in reading. This information is used to suggest alternative teaching strategies in the regular classroom.

5. *Family support team.* A family support team in each school works with parents and community members on issues of parent involvement, attendance, behavior problems, and health and social needs.

6. *Facilitator.* A program facilitator works with teachers to help them implement the reading program, manage the assessments, assist the family support team, improve communication, and help the staff as a whole make certain that every child is making adequate progress.

OUTCOME-BASED EDUCATION SCHOOLS (SPADY)

Transformational Outcome-Based Education (OBE) is designed to equip all students with the knowledge, competence, and orientations needed for them to meet the challenges and opportunities that they will face in their career and family lives after graduating. The OBE model was developed by Dr. William Spady, director of the High Success Program on Outcome-Based Education.

OBE applies four key operating principles to the design, delivery, documentation, and decision-making work of schooling:

1. *Clarity of focus on outcomes of significance.* Culminating demonstrations (outcomes) become the starting point, focal point, and ultimate goal of curriculum design and instruction.

2. *Expanded opportunity and support for learning success.* Time should be used as a flexible resource rather than as a predefined absolute in both the instructional design and delivery to better match differences in student learning rates. Students should have more than one chance to receive needed instruction and to demonstrate success.

3. *High expectations for all to succeed.* Outcomes should represent a high level of challenge for students, and all students should be expected to accomplish them eventually at high performance levels.

4. *Design down from ultimate outcomes.* Curriculum and instructional design should carefully proceed backward from culminating demonstrations (outcomes) on which everything ultimately focuses and rests.

Holt, Rinehart and Winston

Schools employing the OBE model will operate along these dimensions:

1. Decisions, results, and programs will no longer be defined by and limited to specific time blocks and calendar dates.

2. Grading will focus on what students can eventually learn to do well rather than on how well students do the first time they encounter something.

3. There will be a greater emphasis on collaborative models of student learning and the "success for all" principles of OBE.

4. Traditional curriculum structures will be modified to respond to differences in student needs and learning rates.

5. Teachers will focus more on the learning capabilities of their students than on covering the materials in a given time block.

6. Curriculum tracking will disappear, and all instruction will focus on higher-level learning and competencies for all students.

7. There will be far less reliance on norm-reference standardized tests as indicators of either student or teacher accomplishment.

CLASSROOM OF THE FUTURE

The mission of Classroom of the Future is to develop an educational system that prepares students to live and work in the twenty-first century with a commitment and capacity for lifelong learning. The initiative involves designing curricula, instruction, organization, and structure that are appropriate and adaptable for the delivery of education in the future and implementing the design at model demonstration sites. This project has four broad goals:

1. Forecasting the future of American society

2. Identifying education's role in that future

3. Designing curricula, instruction, organization, and structure that are appropriate and necessary to deliver that education in the future

4. Implementing such education at model demonstration sites

There are seven key components of Classroom of the Future:

1. Enabling teaching teams—teams of people, including teachers, tutors, counselors, nurses, psychologists, and others in the school who have positive input to what the youngster is all about—to create a learning community

2. Offering formal and informal staff development

3. Meeting the students' unique needs through individualized instruction and moving students forward as concepts are mastered

4. Focusing curriculum on integrated communications, knowledge, skills, and attitudes necessary for living and constructive citizenship; seeing the connection between the school curriculum and issues facing society; and preparing students for work and lifelong learning

5. Establishing learning as the constant and time as the variable

6. Promoting learning through technology

7. Looking at continuous progress through intelligent planning and involving community members in the planning effort

Holt, Rinehart and Winston

OHIO COMMUNITY LEARNING EXPERIENCE—
NEW AMERICAN SCHOOLS MODEL

The Ohio Community Learning Experience (OCLE) was created by the Ohio Department of Education, in cooperation with Battelle Memorial Institute, as Ohio's plan for implementing New American Schools. Preliminary design work is occurring in fourteen school sites in Ohio.

The OCLE model has four processes and four essential elements that constantly interact with each other:

Processes	Essential Elements
Teaching and learning	Students
Assessment	Teachers
Organizational functions	Content
Governance	Context

These processes and elements have been redefined into a new system—the New American School. New relationships between and among these processes and elements will produce a fundamental shift in the schooling roles of students, teachers, and the wider community. These relationships will also blur distinctions between teachers and students and between schools and communities. The result will be a learning experience that has as its primary purpose the mastery of learning tasks through the integration of schooling with the human and material resources available from the larger community.

The OCLE model has the following learning outcomes:

1. Each learner will demonstrate the ability to recognize, assimilate, and communicate the essential conceptual knowledge, processes, and structures of English, mathematics, science, history, geography, and other academic disciplines.
2. Each learner will demonstrate the ability to apply academic literacy to encounters and interactions within the larger society.
3. Each learner will demonstrate, at increasingly higher levels of rigor and sophistication, the literacy, problem-solving, and application proficiencies necessary to continue learning successfully.
4. Each learner will demonstrate the depth of understanding in each academic discipline (English, mathematics, science, history, geography, and others) necessary to pursue personal goals (e.g., vocational, educational, social, creative, etc.).
5. Each learner will demonstrate understanding of affective, or aesthetic, experiences and of how they promote a complete and well-integrated life.

NORTH CENTRAL ASSOCIATION SCHOOL IMPROVEMENT MODEL

The North Central Association (NCA) School Improvement model provides a framework to help people at the local school level identify their highest-priority needs for student performance gains, to build an improvement plan to raise student performance, and to implement the plan and to document student success.

Based on the belief that all students can learn, the NCA model promotes a continuous improvement process that focuses on enhanced learning for all students.

Basic characteristics of the model include:

1. The school identifies significant learner outcomes that form the basis for the school improvement plan. These outcomes are supported by data and represent complex behaviors.

2. After learner outcomes are identified, data are further analyzed and assembled to provide a student profile relative to each identified outcome. The profile documents that learner outcomes are significant and describes current levels of student growth relative to each outcome.

3. After current levels of student growth are understood, challenging and realistic levels of student learning are determined.

4. The faculty develops a preliminary improvement plan representing the school's design for achieving desired student growth goals.

5. The school assembles a team of peers from outside the school to function as a resource to the school. The team is responsible for:
   - Analyzing the student profile
   - Validating the learner outcomes as significant and appropriate for the school to address
   - Identifying resources that are needed or can be directed to achieve the student outcomes
   - Critiquing the preliminary improvement plan and offering suggestions for enhancement

6. The school finalizes the improvement plan and begins implementation.

7. The school documents student growth throughout the implementation of the plan.

Core Activity

The preceding models contain a range of methods for restructuring and reforming schools. As a future classroom teacher, you no doubt found some ideas that represented the kind of school in which you would feel most comfortable. Based on those ideas, as individuals or in small groups, describe the kind of learning environment that you feel best represents your vision of the "ideal" learning environment. Keep in mind that your vision doesn't necessarily have to look like the present *school building* that we currently use as a learning environment.

MY MODEL FOR IMPROVING "SCHOOLS"

ROLE OF THE TEACHER (describe what the "teacher" does in your model and *who* is the teacher):

ROLE OF THE LEARNER (describe what the "learner" does in your model and *who* is the learner):

CURRICULUM TO BE LEARNED (describe what will be learned in your model and who decides the curriculum):

METHODS OF TEACHING/LEARNING (describe how the curriculum will be taught/learned):

ORGANIZATION OF THE LEARNING ENVIRONMENT (describe how the learning environment will be managed and by whom):

ASSESSMENT OF LEARNING (describe how learning outcomes will be achieved and how successful learning will be determined and by whom):

USE OF RESOURCES (describe the resources that you will need to create a successful learning environment and from where those resources will come):

After you have described or sketched out your model, identify specific characteristics of your model that are derived from the school improvement models you have just read about. Which characteristics are unique to your model?

Compare your model with those created by other individuals or groups in your class. What commonalities did you find? What significant differences? How do you account for these commonalities and differences?

Holt, Rinehart and Winston

SITE-BASED MANAGEMENT

One practice currently associated with Effective School administration is site-based (or school-based) management. Although many schools have used aspects of site-based management for years, it has been only since the mid-1980s that this practice has been articulated holistically as a systematic approach to school management. Essentially, it is an attempt to decentralize decision making in such areas as budgeting, staffing, and curriculum (Martin, 1992). Emerging concomitantly with the emphasis on teacher empowerment, site-based management sought to implement a "grass-roots" decision-making model. Teachers would have an integral role in determining how resources were allocated, which staff development activities were planned and implemented, and who controlled curriculum changes in each building. Many of the practices associated with site-based management, in fact, were quite similar to those found in the literature on Effective Schools and restructuring (Martin, 1992; Griswold, 1992).

One of the primary earmarks of site-based management is participatory decision making. Virtually all models recommend that the building principal and the teachers be most heavily involved in the process, whereas other models would include parents, students, and central office administrators. Most advocates would agree that the larger, most encompassing decisions of the district should be made at the central office level, but issues involving *how* policies are implemented should be left to the individual buildings (Martin, 1992). In citing Lawson (1989), Martin argues that "(a) those most closely affected by decisions should play a significant role in making them and (b) educational change will be most effective and long lasting when carried out by people who feel ownership and responsibility for the process" (p. 21).

These assumptions reflect nine guiding research principles:

1. A school is the primary unit of change.
2. A healthy school climate is an important prerequisite for effective improvement.
3. A high level of trust, open communication, and a concern for people promote effective school improvement efforts.
4. Significant and lasting school improvement takes considerable planning time and effort.
5. School improvement requires personal and group commitment to new and higher performance levels.
6. Teachers and principals must believe that all students can master the basic learning objectives of the school.
7. The role of the principal is the key to effective school change.
8. Efforts to change schools are most effective when they have been focused on influencing the entire school culture in a risk-free, collegial atmosphere.
9. Change in the total organization of a school is fostered through teacher participation in project planning and implementation with strong achievement, encouragement, commitment, and acceptance of results by supervisors (Martin, 1992, p. 22).

In your observations in schools you may become aware of a site-based or a school-based management system in operation. Try to identify what the teachers and principal are doing to implement practices such as those discussed earlier. Further,

Holt, Rinehart and Winston

try to determine if characteristics of effective and/or restructured schools exist in the building and if the site-based system is essentially an outgrowth of either or both of these concepts. Finally, in your Journal Entry and in your class discussions, focus upon how change occurs in schools and whether these changes are largely reactive (i.e., the result of some external pressure) or proactive (i.e., the result of a school staff's desire to create an effective learning environment).

PROFESSIONAL DEVELOPMENT SCHOOLS

Since the late 1980s teacher education programs and pre K–12 schools have been working together to help prepare preservice teachers and to provide ongoing professional development to practicing teachers. Dubbed "professional development schools" (PDS), these partnerships first appeared as a recommendation of the Holmes Group, which was a collection of research-oriented institutions of higher education that also had some commitment to teacher education. The concept was further endorsed by John Goodlad in a set of "postulates" that he proposed to reconceptualize the process of teacher education. More recently, the Holmes Group has expanded its base to include institutions with a strong tradition of preparing teachers along with local education associations (LEAs) that have also been interested in restructuring the manner in which they provide staff development for their existing teaching staff. This expanded group is called the Holmes Partnership, and it is encouraging the creation of ongoing collaborative relationships between teacher preparation institutions and LEAs.

The PDS partnerships have been described as "exemplars of practice, builders of knowledge, and vehicles for sharing professional learning among educators with an emphasis on putting research into practice and practice into research" (Metcalf-Turner and Fischetti, 1996). In a sense, what this model is attempting to do is to "simultaneously renew" pre K–12 schools and programs of teacher education. Supporters of PDS point out that it does little good to reform schools if we continue to turn out traditional teachers or to develop innovative teachers and then place them into ineffective schools.

Supporters of PDS also suggest that the assumption that one becomes a teacher after completing a teacher preparation program is erroneous. A teacher is always in the process of *becoming* a teacher throughout his or her career. The concept of ongoing professional development beginning with (a) the preservice teacher preparation program in conjunction with (b) a strong liberal arts background and (c) continuing through entry-year or fifth-year "induction" into the profession and (d) culminating with a career-long commitment to ongoing professional growth is an essential element of PDS.

Your teacher preparation program may be part of a PDS partnership, or it may be in the process of developing some relationships on a formal or informal basis. Some common elements of these types of relationships include:

- Teamlike organizational structure with four to five classroom teachers, two to three university professors, five to ten graduate interns, several teacher candidates, and others with appropriate areas of expertise serving as resource people (Metcalf-Turner and Fischetti, 1996)

- Long-term, ongoing field placement at a particular site that exemplifies "best practices" and involves teacher candidates as part of a teaching team in the school
- On-site teaching by university faculty and/or adjunct faculty from the LEA and a concomitant exchange in which classroom teachers provide on-campus learning experiences
- Assessment of teacher candidates' learning through a variety of strategies appropriate to that site and to the needs of the candidates
- An ongoing commitment of the college to the PDS so that the partnership ultimately benefits the community and enhances the achievement of the students in the pre K–12 setting

Although this list is hardly exhaustive, it does represent some of the major premises upon which PDS partnerships are built. As a result, both the college faculty and the classroom teachers should experience considerable growth in their own teaching skills, increased understanding of the art and science of teaching, and an improved appreciation for each other's areas of expertise.

As you begin your journey toward becoming a teacher, it is essential that you understand that you will never stop learning. In terms of your preservice teacher preparation and the school(s) in which you find yourself teaching, you should choose situations that encourage high-quality professional development. The National Foundation for the Improvement of Education (NFIE, 1996) has summarized the characteristics of a high-quality professional development program as follows:

- Has the goal of improving student learning at the heart of every school endeavor
- Helps teachers and other school staff meet the future needs of students who learn in different ways and who come from diverse cultural, linguistic, and socioeconomic backgrounds
- Provides adequate time for inquiry, reflection, and mentoring and is an important part of the normal working day of all public school educators
- Is rigorous, sustained, and adequate to the long-term change of practice
- Is directed toward teachers' intellectual development and leadership
- Fosters a deepening of subject-matter knowledge, a greater understanding of learning, and a greater appreciation of students' needs
- Is designed and directed by teachers, incorporates the best principles of adult learning, and involves shared decisions designed to improve the school
- Balances individual priorities with school and district needs and advances the profession as a whole
- Makes the best use of new technologies
- Is site-based and supportive of a clearly articulated vision for students

An important aspect of your exploration of the teaching profession should be the examination of your own education and how well you are prepared to continue learning throughout your career. As part of your discussion of professional development with your campus-based instructor, your classmates, your cooperating teacher(s), and others enrolled in the program, you may want to seek answers to the following questions:

Suggested Activity 1

EXPLORING YOUR OWN PROFESSIONAL DEVELOPMENT

---

1. What opportunities do you have in your teacher preparation program to observe and interview practicing teachers?
2. How central is the process of "reflective teaching" to the clinical and field experiences in which you are required to participate?
3. When in your program do you encounter a practicing teacher who serves as your mentor?
4. How *connected* are your field experiences with each other, and how *integrated* are they with your campus-based activities?
5. How is your learning assessed, and how do you learn to assess the outcomes established for your students?
6. What options for professional development do you have after completing your teacher preparation program and receiving your teaching license/certificate?
7. How do your mentor teacher/cooperating teachers keep themselves up-to-date professionally? What have been their most satisfying and useful professional development experiences since they became teachers?

Questions for Discussion

1. Is it possible to judge a school's commitment to reforming/restructuring on the basis of your observations? What information did you feel was missing, and how would you go about gathering that information?
2. Did you agree with the criteria for judging school reforming/restructuring discussed in this chapter? What criteria would you add or delete?
3. According to the information that you and your classmates gathered, how does your ideal learning environment differ from existing schools? What ways would you suggest to improve existing schools? What problems would you have teaching in a school that you judged to be uncommitted to reforming/restructuring?
4. Should schools be restructured, especially if they are determined by research to be operating ineffectively? Has society changed sufficiently in the past ten years to warrant restructuring schools whether the schools are operating effectively or not?
5. How might you use the activities in this chapter to help you in adjusting to the school in which you do your practice teaching? How might they help you to select the school in which you take your first teaching job? In judging your children's school as a parent?
6. How can schools encourage teachers to continue to develop as professionals? How should colleges be involved in this process?

References

Good, T., and Brophy, J. (1973). *Looking in classrooms*. New York: Harper & Row.

Griswold, Maggie M. (August 1992). Exploration of restructuring in learning goals: A search for departures in student learning experience in a program for at-risk students. Unpublished doctoral dissertation, Bowling Green State University.

Holt, Rinehart and Winston

Jencks, C. L., Smith, M., Acland, H., Bane, M. S., Cohen, D. K., Gintis, H., Heyns, B. L., and Michaelson, S. (1972). *Inequality: A reassessment of the effects of family and schooling in America*. New York: Basic Books.

Martin, Barry N. (August 1992). Factors related to teacher perceptions of the elementary principal's role in the school-based management process. Unpublished doctoral dissertation, Bowling Green State University.

Metcalf-Turner, P., and Fischetti, J. (September–October 1996). Professional development schools: Persisting questions and lessons learned. *Journal of Teacher Education*, 292-299.

National Foundation for the Improvement of Education. (1996). *Teachers take charge of their learning*: *Transforming professional development for student success* (p. xv). Washington, D.C.

Ohio Department of Education. (1996). School improvement models. Unpublished document provided by the Ohio Department of Education to Venture Capital Schools.

Purkey, S. C., and Smith, M. S. (March 1983). Effective schools: A review. *The Elementary School Journal* 83 (4).

Rosenthal, R., and Jacobson, L. (1968). *Pygmalion in the classroom: Teacher expectation and pupils' intellectual development*. New York: Holt, Rinehart and Winston.

Rowan, B., Bossert, S. T., and Dwyer, D. C. (April 1983). Research on effective schools: A cautionary note. *Educational Researcher*, 24-31.

Sizer, T. R. (1984). *Horace's compromise: The dilemma of the American high school*. Boston: Houghton Mifflin.

Weber, G. (1971). *Inner city children can be taught to read: Four successful schools*. (Occasional Paper No. 17). Washington, D.C.: Council for Basic Education.

Chapter 4

OBSERVING CLASSROOM INTERACTION

In Chapters 2 and 3 we placed you into the context of a specific school and class-room and had you focus primarily on the physical and noninteractive dimensions of school and classroom phenomena: seating arrangements, a description of a teacher's day, the location of various types of resource rooms, and so on. In this chapter, the observing becomes a bit more challenging as we focus your attention onto various dynamic/interactive aspects of classroom life. A wide range of interactions occurs daily between teachers and students, and from this wide range we have selected a set of interactions that meshes neatly with the major objective of this chapter.

Our major objective in this chapter is to put you in touch with the major ele-ments of the contemporary teacher's day and role, namely lesson planning, lesson implementation (teaching), and classroom management, and to do so in a manner that sharpens your classroom observational skills. Planning, teaching, and evaluating lessons are the basic stuff of a teacher's career, and to aspire to become a teacher suggests that you want to be deeply involved with these basic teacher tasks. To help you be sure that this is the case, our Core Activity will give you the opportunity to observe several lessons from teachers with differing levels of experience. Our focus will be on veteran teachers as well as on those relatively new to the profession—teachers who have two to five years of experience. This type of exposure should provide you with some valuable developmental insights regarding the career of teaching. Although observing teachers in the beginning phase of their career should prove illuminating, this activity will be quite productive if all observations are done with veteran teachers. Some students might also find it interesting to observe stu-dent or first-year teachers.

Beyond the Core Activity, we offer seven carefully conceived activities that cover a wide range of interactive classroom situations. Each of these activities has a slightly different contribution to make to your overall awareness of the interactive nature of teaching and the complex nature of the classroom teacher's role. The Sug-gested Activities will place you into a position to code various forms of praise as they occur within several lessons, to classify different types of questions, and to ob-serve transition periods, classroom management, learning climates, cooperative learning, and the use of technology in the classroom. Although each of the activities in this chapter has its own introduction, a general suggestion pertaining to teacher expectations may enrich the observations that occur in several of these activities. Since the 1960s evidence has suggested that teachers' beliefs about certain cate-

Holt, Rinehart and Winston

gories of students (low achievers, slow learners, etc.) will help shape the teachers' expectations about the learning potential of students whom teachers place into these socially constructed categories. These expectations, in turn, will influence the ways that teachers interact with these students. When teachers' expectations for student achievement are inaccurate, it is quite likely that inappropriate teacher-student interaction will result. More specifically, the students on the low end of the expectation continuum could receive less opportunity to respond to higher-level questioning, receive individual help and praise, have the teacher listen patiently to their responses, and so on (Brophy, 1983; Good, 1987). In the educational literature, the phenomenon of teacher beliefs leading to behaviors that create the classroom realities that correspond to the original belief is called the *self-fulfilling prophecy*. Although the evidence that has accrued regarding the self-fulfilling prophecy has been interpreted differently by some academics (Rist, 1987; Wineburg, 1987), many K–12 practitioners and teacher educators accept the proposition that what teachers believe about the learning potential of individual students is quite important.

For the purpose of maximizing your observation opportunities in this chapter, as you carry out specific observational tasks, you should also watch for differential patterns of teacher praise, teacher listening, teacher questioning, teacher touching, and teacher proximity (getting close to students). As you discuss your data and impressions with fellow students you may find that the patterns associated with negative self-fulfilling prophecies appear to be alive and well in certain classrooms. This, in turn, may lead to inquiries regarding staff development programs that aim to countervail the tendency toward negative self-fulfilling prophecies. If this occurs, a program worthy of your attention is called Teacher Expectations and Student Achievement (TESA). Since 1971 educators representing approximately four thousand educational agencies across the United States have received TESA training. More information about TESA can be had by writing to: TESA Program Director, Los Angeles County Office of Education, 9300 Imperial Highway, Downey, CA 90242-2890. With this suggestion made, let us now turn to the Core Activity.

ACTIVITIES FOR CHAPTER 4

The Core Activity (Lesson Observation)

As a prospective teacher you should appreciate the fact that you will plan and teach thousands of lessons during the course of your teaching career. In addition, a significant portion of the teacher education program that prepares you for your career will be devoted to teaching you how to plan, implement, and evaluate lessons. This is a logical approach since planning and teaching lessons comprise at least two-thirds of the real work of teaching. Being so, they are critical activities for prospective teachers to observe and contemplate. When professionals state that teaching is hard work, they typically have in mind the detailed thinking that precedes many lessons and the large amounts of energy needed to enthusiastically deliver six to ten lessons a day.

Because of the fundamental importance of lesson planning and implementation, in this activity you will have the opportunity to observe as many lessons as possible from two kinds of teachers. First, you will observe and discuss lesson planning with veteran teachers (teachers who have been teaching for five or more years), and then you may choose to observe a recommended teacher who has less experience. Comparing and contrasting lessons taught by these teachers should help you to appreciate, first, not only that lesson planning and implementation are critical aspects of a teacher's career at all phases, but also that they are done differently at different phases in a teacher's career. If you do not find this aspect of a teacher's role intriguing, it may be a sign that teaching is not the right career for you.

The Observation Task(s)

On the pages immediately following, there are two classroom observation forms—one form to be used with a veteran teacher, and a second form to be used with either a veteran teacher or a relatively new teacher. Your task is to observe these teachers as they deliver a similar (not identical) type of lesson to a similar group of students in the same, or nearly the same, grade level and to answer some questions on the forms during and after the lesson. You should complete as many observations as possible, making duplicate copies of the forms as needed. You will note that a number of questions tie in to the information on effective schools in the earlier chapter. If time permits, you should ask the observed teachers some questions about the lessons that you have observed.

Holt, Rinehart and Winston

Core Activity

LESSON OBSERVATION FORM
(EXPERIENCED TEACHER)

Your Name: _____   Participating Teacher: _____

Date: _____   Grade/Subject: _____   School: _____

DURING THE LESSON

1. At the beginning of the lesson, did the teacher do anything to get the attention of the class? If "yes," please describe.

   _____

   _____

   _____

2. At the beginning, or sometime during the lesson, did the teacher do something to get the students interested in the lesson that they were about to experience? If "yes," please describe.

   _____

   _____

   _____

3. What was the teacher's main instructional objective in this lesson (the skill or knowledge, etc., that he or she was most interested in having the students learn)?

   _____

   _____

   _____

   _____

4. What did the students learn in this lesson?

   _____

   _____

   _____

   _____

5. What were the students' reactions to the lesson (observe the class as a whole as well as two specific students)?

   (a) The whole class:_____

   _____

   _____

   (b) The two individuals:_____

   _____

   _____

6. Did the teacher in any way provide for individual differences? If "yes," please describe.

   _____

   _____

   _____

   _____

7. In what specific ways did the teacher either praise the students or communicate high expectations to them?

   _____

   _____

   _____

   _____

8. During the lesson, did the students have the opportunity to interact with each other in dyads, triads, or in larger groups? If "yes," what did they do, and what do you suppose was the purpose of the student-to-student interaction?

   _____

   _____

   _____

   _____

9. What were some of the materials or visual aids that the teacher used during the lesson (examples: chalkboard, posters, pictures, audiotapes or videotapes, movies, computers, etc.)?

_____

_____

_____

10. How exactly did the teacher close the lesson?

_____

_____

_____

11. What evidence did you see that suggested that the main instructional objective of this lesson had been achieved?

_____

_____

_____

_____

AFTER THE LESSON

1. What did you like about the way that this lesson was taught?

_____

_____

_____

2. If you were going to teach this lesson to a similar group of students, what, if anything, would you change in the way that this lesson was taught, and for what reason(s)?

_____

_____

_____

_____

3. What questions do you have about the way that the lesson was presented?

_____

_____

_____

_____

_____

If you were able to speak to the teacher after the lesson, answer the following questions:

4. Did this lesson introduce new material, or was it a review lesson?

_____

_____

_____

_____

5. Did the teacher have a written lesson plan or some type of written notes to guide his or her instruction during the lesson? If "yes," please describe the written notes. Were they in a lesson plan book, on a separate sheet of paper in a lesson plan format, on an index card, or the like?

_____

_____

_____

_____

6. From where did the content for this lesson come?

❑ teacher's original research/lesson design   ❑ a textbook

❑ a curriculum guide   ❑ one or more of these

❑ the Internet

Core Activity
LESSON OBSERVATION FORM
(NEW TEACHER)

Your Name: _____ Participating Teacher: _____

Date: _____ Grade/Subject: _____ School: _____

DURING THE LESSON

1. At the beginning of the lesson, did the teacher do anything to get the attention of the class? If "yes," please describe.

   _____

   _____

   _____

2. At the beginning, or sometime during the lesson, did the teacher do something to get the students interested in the lesson that they were about to experience? If "yes," please describe.

   _____

   _____

   _____

3. What was the teacher's main instructional objective in this lesson (the skill or knowledge, etc., that he or she was most interested in having the students learn)?

   _____

   _____

   _____

   _____

4. What did the students learn in this lesson?

   _____

   _____

   _____

   _____

Holt, Rinehart and Winston

5. What were the students' reactions to the lesson (observe the class as a whole as well as two specific students)?

   (a) The whole class:_____

   _____

   _____

   _____

   (b) The two individuals:_____

   _____

   _____

   _____

6. Did the teacher in any way provide for individual differences? If "yes," please describe.

   _____

   _____

   _____

7. In what specific ways did the teacher either praise the students or communicate high expectations to them?

   _____

   _____

   _____

   _____

8. During the lesson did the students have the opportunity to interact with each other in dyads, triads, or in larger groups? If "yes," what did they do, and what do you suppose was the purpose of the student-to-student interaction?

   _____

   _____

   _____

   _____

9. What were some of the materials or visual aids that the teacher used during the lesson (examples: chalkboard, posters, pictures, audiotapes or videotapes, movies, computers, etc.)?

_____

_____

_____

10. How exactly did the teacher close the lesson?

_____

_____

_____

11. What evidence did you see that suggested that the main instructional objective of this lesson was achieved?

_____

_____

_____

_____

AFTER THE LESSON

1. What did you like about the way that this lesson was taught?

_____

_____

_____

2. If you were going to teach this lesson to a similar group of students, what, if anything, would you change in the way that this lesson was taught, and for what reasons?

_____

_____

_____

_____

3. What questions do you have about the way that the lesson was presented?

_____

_____

_____

_____

If you were able to speak to the teacher after the lesson, answer the following questions:

4. Did this lesson introduce new material, or was it a review lesson?

_____

_____

_____

_____

5. Did the teacher have a written lesson plan or some type of written notes to guide his or her instruction during the lesson? If "yes," please describe the written notes. Were they in a lesson plan book, on a separate sheet of paper in a lesson plan format, on an index card, or the like?

_____

_____

_____

_____

6. From where did the content for this lesson come?
    ❑ teacher's original research/lesson design   ❑ a textbook
    ❑ a curriculum guide   ❑ one or more of these
    ❑ the Internet

COMPARISON/CONTRAST QUESTIONS

1. What differences, in any, did you note between:

    (a) the way the two teachers planned their lessons?

    _____

    _____

    _____

    (b) the way the two teachers taught their lessons?

    _____

    _____

    _____

2. What, if anything, did the two teachers have in common?

    _____

    _____

    _____

3. From this set of observations, what did you discover/learn that was:

    (a) Interesting?_____

    _____

    _____

    (b) Unanticipated?_____

    _____

    _____

    _____

Holt, Rinehart and Winston

Increasingly, students, teachers, and in-service teachers are being asked to play a role in the professional development of another student teacher or in-service teacher. Sometimes this new "staff development" role involves observing a live or videotaped teaching episode. Activity 1 provides you with a simple, flexible observation instrument that will place you in a position to collect and communicate useful data about student/teacher interaction in various types of lessons.

Please note that we have provided three different interaction observation forms for use in classrooms with different seating arrangements. We have also included a fourth blank form because we expect that some of you will have to draw up your own seating chart to complete this activity. Although in our task each symbol equals a specific teacher behavior, it should be well understood that at a later time you can modify the symbol system to allow you to focus on other teacher behaviors. For example, the minus sign ($-$) could stand for students who call out an answer without raising their hand, or it could stand for students who answer questions; a plus sign ($+$) could stand for students who answer questions and receive praise. In a similar vein, this seating chart and symbol system could be used to compare the amount of teacher praise (and so on) that was received by boys as opposed to by girls during a lesson.

THE TASK

Arrange to observe a teacher or student teacher who is teaching a large-group (whole-class) lesson in mathematics, social studies, English, and so on, and then follow the instructions listed next. Use the form that most closely approximates the seating arrangement in the classroom in which you are observing, or make up a new form on which to collect data if the seating arrangement in your room is divergent/unique.

INSTRUCTIONS FOR USING THE TEACHER/STUDENT
INTERACTION OBSERVATION FORM

1. Observe the first twenty to thirty minutes of a particular lesson.
2. Familiarize yourself with the symbols listed next and with where to place the symbols in the seating chart:
   (a) The dot (●) will go into Box 1. Put a dot into the box when the teacher has given the student a chance to:
      (1) answer a question
      (2) give a report
      (3) receive help from a teacher
   (b) The minus ($-$) signs will go into Box 2. Put a minus sign into Box 2 when the teacher requests or demands that a specific child stop doing something. (This is often referred to as "desist" in the literature.)
   (c) The plus signs ($+$) will go into Box 3. Put a plus sign into Box 3 when a student receives praise that is related to managing his or her behavior.
   (d) The checks ($\sqrt{}$) will go into Box 4. Put a check into Box 4 when a student receives praise for instruction-related work.

3. Occasionally the teacher will give the entire class or a specific group praise or the opportunity to respond as an entire group. Use the boxes that follow the seating chart to record these whole-class or small-group behaviors.

   (a) Put an *X* into the "total class responses" box when the teacher asks for a total class response.

   (b) Put an *X* into the "entire class receives praise" box when this occurs.

4. On the seating chart, signify whether a boy or a girl is seated there by putting a *B* or a *G* above the box. At a later point, you will count up and analyze the data in terms of gender, if indeed you wish to do that. Other letters, of course, could be used to indicate ethnicity if you were interested in coding and quantifying that aspect of classroom interaction.

5. Fill out the comments portion of the Interaction Observation Form.

TEACHER/STUDENT INTERACTION OBSERVATION FORM 1

Teacher's Name: _____   Lesson Began: _____

Observer's Name: _____   Lesson Ended: _____

Date: _____   Lesson Content: _____

(Math, reading, etc.)

(Front of Room)

Row 1	Row 2	Row 3	Row 4	Row 5	Row 6	Row 7

(Box #)

1	2
3	4

| Opportunity for total class Response (X) | Entire Class Receives Praise (X) | |

The Code

● = Student has opportunity to answer question, give a report, or receive help from the teacher (Box 1)

− = Teacher asks student to stop doing something (Box 2)

+ = Student receives praise related to managing his or her behavior (Box 3)

√ = Student receives praise that reinforces instruction (Box 4)

Holt, Rinehart and Winston

TEACHER/STUDENT INTERACTION OBSERVATION FORM 2

Teacher's Name: _____   Lesson Began: _____

Observer's Name: _____   Lesson Ended: _____

Date: _____   Lesson Content: _____
                                                      (Math, reading, etc.)

(Front of Room)

Row 1	Row 2	Row 3	Row 4	Row 5	Row 6	Row 7

(Box #)

1	2
3	4

Opportunity for total class
Response (X)

Entire Class Receives
Praise (X)

The Code
- ● = Student has opportunity to answer question, give a report, or receive help from the teacher (Box 1)
- − = Teacher asks student to stop doing something (Box 2)
- + = Student receives praise related to managing his or her behavior (Box 3)
- √ = Student receives praise that reinforces instruction (Box 4)

Holt, Rinehart and Winston

TEACHER/STUDENT INTERACTION OBSERVATION FORM 3

Teacher's Name: _____   Lesson Began: _____

Observer's Name: _____   Lesson Ended: _____

Date: _____   Lesson Content: _____
                                                 (Math, reading, etc.)

(Front of Room)

Row 1	Row 2	Row 3	Row 4	Row 5	Row 6	Row 7

(Box #)

1	2
3	4

Opportunity for total class   Entire Class Receives
Response (X)   Praise (X)

The Code
- ● = Student has opportunity to answer question, give a report, or receive help from the teacher (Box 1)
- − = Teacher asks student to stop doing something (Box 2)
- + = Student receives praise related to managing his or her behavior (Box 3)
- √ = Student receives praise that reinforces instruction (Box 4)

Holt, Rinehart and Winston

TEACHER/STUDENT INTERACTION OBSERVATION FORM 4

Teacher's Name: _____   Lesson Began: _____

Observer's Name: _____   Lesson Ended: _____

Date: _____   Lesson Content: _____
                                                          (Math, reading, etc.)

(Front of Room)

Opportunity for total class
Response (X)

Entire Class Receives
Praise (X)

(Box #)

1	2
3	4

The Code

   ● = Student has opportunity to answer question, give a report, or receive help
    from the teacher (Box 1)

   − = Teacher asks student to stop doing something (Box 2)

   + = Student receives praise related to managing his or her behavior (Box 3)

   √ = Student receives praise that reinforces instruction (Box 4)

Holt, Rinehart and Winston

Observer's Name:_____ Date:_____

1. Comments about the distribution of opportunity to respond, desist, and praise during the lesson:

    _____

    _____

    _____

    _____

    _____

    _____

    _____

    _____

2. Assuming that you were the principal of the school or this student teacher's college supervisor, what questions might you raise with the teacher or student teacher if you had observed ten lessons by this teacher and recorded interaction patterns very similar to those that you observed today?

    _____

    _____

    _____

    _____

    _____

    _____

    _____

    _____

Suggested Activity 2
TRANSITION PERIODS

Although it is quite appropriate to draw your attention to classroom lessons and to the management problems that sometimes occur during lessons, it is also appropriate to more fully reveal to you the responsibilities of a classroom teacher in an observational activity related to transitional periods—the times before, after, and between lessons and other organized activities. The questions and check-off items on the Transition Period Observation Form will clarify a number of things for you; first, that there is more to teaching than lesson planning, implementation, and evaluation and, second, that the organizational aspects of transition periods are quite worthy of your consideration. Indeed, time saved during a routine or transition period is time that can be used to provide greater opportunities for academic learning.

Before using the transition period form, some examples of transition period times and activities should prove helpful. For example, during the elementary school day in between lessons you might see a teacher walk her class to the playground for a physical education activity or to the bathroom for a "watering" break. You might also see the students given a few minutes of free (decision-making) time or time to organize their homework packets to take home or to prepare for the teacher's inspection. Similarly, you might also see an elementary, junior high, or high school teacher taking roll, checking homework, lining students up for lunch or dismissal, or simply telling students to turn to a specific page in a certain textbook and then to look up when they are ready for the next lesson.

Use the Transition Period Observation Form on the same days that you carry out your Core Activity or Suggested Activity 1 to observe the way that teachers manage time during transition periods. This form can be used for observations at any time of the day because lessons are always beginning and ending with transitions occurring before and after. Interestingly, research has demonstrated that teachers vary widely in their ability to efficiently organize their transition periods.

Holt, Rinehart and Winston

TRANSITION PERIOD OBSERVATION FORM*

Your Name: _____ Participating Teacher: _____

Date: _____ Grade/Subject: _____ School: _____

1. During the transition or routine does the teacher do things that students could do for themselves?

   _____

   _____

   _____

2. Does the teacher give clear instructions about what to do next before moving into a transition period?

   _____

   _____

   _____

3. Is the transition period routine (taking attendance, lining up to sharpen pencils, moving to another seating arrangement, etc.) organized in a time-efficient manner, or can a more time-efficient manner be developed?

   _____

   _____

   _____

4. Does the teacher circulate during transitions to handle individual needs? Does he or she take care of these before attempting to begin a new activity?

   _____

   _____

   _____

   _____

5. Does the teacher signal the end of a transition and the beginning of a structured activity properly and quickly gain everyone's attention?

   _____

   _____

   _____

---

*Adaptation of two forms from *Looking in Classrooms* (4th ed.) by T. L. Good and J. E. Brophy, 1987, Harper & Row. Reprinted by permission of the publisher.

6. Does the teacher use singing, background music, or any other creative device to add interest to the transition period/routine?

_____

_____

_____

_____

Check if applicable:

_____ 1. Transitions occur too abruptly for students because the teacher fails to give advance warning or to finish up reminders when needed.

_____ 2. The teacher insists on unnecessary rituals or formalisms that cause delays or disruptions.

_____ 3. The teacher is interrupted by individuals with the same problem or request; this could be handled by establishing a general rule or procedure (describe).

_____ 4. Delays occur because frequently used materials are stored in hard-to-reach places.

_____ 5. Poor traffic patterns result in pushing, bumping, or unnecessary noise.

_____ 6. Delays occur while the teacher prepares equipment or illustrates what should have been prepared earlier.

_____ 7. Behavioral problems occur because of lack of structure during transition or because of other unidentified reasons.

Suggested Activity 3

CLASSROOM MANAGEMENT

Classroom managing and effective teaching are like breathing and exhaling: They are inextricably intertwined, part of an ongoing process, but are often considered and discussed as separate processes. Indeed, for most teachers the words *classroom management* and *teaching* point to different areas of a teacher's responsibilities.

Further, in college teacher education programs one will often find one specific course on classroom management and several courses on instruction of one kind or another. The classroom management course is considered critical and will usually contain readings, lectures, and discussions about how to create and maintain good student behavior; arrange your classroom to promote effective instruction; get off to a good start at the beginning of the year; and organize and manage the flow of information and paper that occurs before, during, and after instruction. Classroom management, in short, is about all the little and big things (tactics and strategies) that teachers do to create a learning environment in which learning occurs smoothly and efficiently for a wide range of learners.

In recent years educational research has validated a number of logical ideas about classroom management. For example, regarding good room arrangement, student teachers are taught to keep high-traffic areas free of congestion, be sure that all students are easily seen by the teacher, and be sure that all students can easily see instructional presentations. In a related vein, a consensus has grown around the use of rules in both elementary and secondary settings. Today, student teachers are taught how to develop a set of rules with their students and are usually told to keep the number of rules to somewhere between five and eight.

Although education research has provided a set of validated tactics and strategies for classroom management, it is also true that teachers will always encounter behavioral situations that require special data collection, thought, and solutions. Any exposure to these types of problems will make it clear that the teaching profession needs bright people who can collect and analyze data in unique situations and come up with a variety of possible solutions and plans of action.

The four observation forms provided in Suggested Activity 3 allow you to observe classroom management from several vantage points. These forms can be used individually or together. For example, you might start with Form A and note that a particular student is a significant behavior problem. In some elementary and in most secondary settings, you could choose to observe this same student in one or more different classrooms. Form B, which focuses on the effects that different teachers have on the same student, may prove helpful here, particularly if you are in a secondary school setting. In the same vein, Form C, which helps you collect case study data on the student in one or more classrooms, provides another interesting type of data. Form D, which focuses on off-task and on-task behavior, is another good source of case study data. Please note that the observation activities focus on the student behavior aspect of classroom management. As indicated, classroom management is concerned with a wide-ranging set of classroom conditions and factors, all of which influence student behavior and learning. As you observe and interview throughout various chapters in this text, you should maintain an active curiosity about classroom management.

You can begin this activity with Form A and observe in three or four classrooms before choosing to use Forms B, C, or D. You might also choose to start with Form A and use that form for all of your observations.

Holt, Rinehart and Winston

CLASSROOM MANAGEMENT OBSERVATION FORM A

Your Name: _____ Participating Teacher: _____

Date: _____ Grade/Subject: _____ School: _____

Focus: Classroom management in one classroom

Data Collection

1. Did you notice any behavioral problems in this classroom? If "yes," please describe.

   _____

   _____

   _____

2. How did the teacher respond to these problems?

   _____

   _____

   _____

3. What was the student's or students' immediate response to the teacher's interaction?

   _____

   _____

   _____

4. During the lesson did the teacher make positive statements to the whole class or to individual students to reward and encourage appropriate behavior? If "yes," include some of these positive statements:

   _____

   _____

   _____

   _____

Holt, Rinehart and Winston

5. Did the teacher use what you would consider to be negative measures in response to student misbehavior? If so, please describe these measures:

_____

_____

_____

_____

_____

Analysis

(a) During this observation period, which management techniques appeared to be most effective?

_____

_____

_____

(b) Which techniques, if any, appeared problematical or ineffective to you? What questions do you have about these techniques?

_____

_____

_____

_____

_____

CLASSROOM MANAGEMENT OBSERVATION FORM B

Your Name:_____ Participating Teacher:_____

Date: _____ Grade/Subject: _____School: _____

Focus: The behavior of one student in several classrooms

Data Collection

Observe one student's reactions in two or three different classes, noting his or her participation, facial expressions, body language, involvement in class, and relationships with peers and teachers.

1. How are these classrooms alike, and how are they different?

    _____

    _____

    _____

    _____

2. Is the mix of students roughly the same in all the classes, and if not, how are the classes different?

    _____

    _____

    _____

3. Does the student's behavior change from class to class? If "yes," describe the change.

    _____

    _____

    _____

    _____

4. Does the change in behavior, either positive or negative, appear to be triggered by specific teacher behaviors? If "yes," what teacher behaviors appear to be associated with the change in student behavior?

    _____

    _____

    _____

Holt, Rinehart and Winston

5. Is there any chance that your student's behavior change might be linked to the subject matter being taught? If "yes," why do you think this *might* be the case?

_____

_____

_____

6. Are there any other possible explanations for the student's behavior? If "yes," please spell out competing explanations that *might* be involved.

_____

_____

_____

7. What do different teachers do to encourage effective communication with the student you are observing as well as with other students?

_____

_____

_____

_____

8. What do you see teachers doing that appears to inhibit effective communication?

_____

_____

_____

_____

_____

_____

_____

_____

_____

_____

Analysis

If you were a school counselor providing suggestions to all of the teachers with whom this student interacted, what suggestions might you provide?

_____

_____

_____

_____

_____

_____

_____

_____

CLASSROOM MANAGEMENT OBSERVATION FORM C

Your Name:_____ Participating Teacher:_____

Date:_____ Grade/Subject:_____ School:_____

Focus: A case study of a specific student's classroom behavior*

Data Collection (Part 1)

Use the codes on this form (A—Student Behavior and B—Apparent Cause) to record the student's behavior at five-minute intervals and link it to antecedent causes when possible. Observe the student with more than one teacher and in more than one instructional setting before filling out Part 2 of Form C.

	TIME	A	B	A.	STUDENT BEHAVIOR
1.	_____	_____	_____	a.	Pays attention or actively works at assignment
2.	_____	_____	_____	b.	Stares into space or closes eyes
3.	_____	_____	_____	c.	Fidgets, taps, amuses self
4.	_____	_____	_____	d.	Distracts others—entertains, jokes
5.	_____	_____	_____	e.	Distracts others—questions, seeks help
6.	_____	_____	_____	f.	Investigates
7.	_____	_____	_____	g.	Distracts others—attacks or teases
8.	_____	_____	_____	h.	Leaves seat—goes to teacher
9.	_____	_____	_____	i.	Leaves seat—wanders, runs, plays
10.	_____	_____	_____	j.	Leaves seat—does approved action (what?)
11.	_____	_____	_____	k.	Leaves seat—does forbidden action (what?)
12.	_____	_____	_____	l.	Calls out answer
13.	_____	_____	_____	m.	Calls out irrelevant comment (what?)
14.	_____	_____	_____	n.	Calls out comment about teacher (what?)
15.	_____	_____	_____	o.	Deliberately causes disruption
16.	_____	_____	_____	p.	Destroys property (whose? what?)
17.	_____	_____	_____	q.	Leaves room without permission
18.	_____	_____	_____	r.	Other (specify)

---

*Please note that this activity will have to be cleared by the principal who will direct you toward specific classrooms.

Holt, Rinehart and Winston

B.   APPARENT CAUSE

What triggers the behavior?

19. _____ _____ _____   a. No observable cause—suddenly begins acting out

20. _____ _____ _____   b. Appears stumped/frustrated and gives up

21. _____ _____ _____   c. Finishes work, has nothing to do

22. _____ _____ _____   d. Distracted/bothered by classmate (who?)

23. _____ _____ _____   e. Asked to respond or perform by teacher

24. _____ _____ _____   f. Teacher checked or asked about progress on assigned work

25. _____ _____ _____   g. Teacher calls for attention or return to work

26. _____ _____ _____   h. Teacher praise (for what?)

27. _____ _____ _____   i. Teacher criticism (for what?)

28. _____ _____ _____   j. Teacher praises or rewards another student

29. _____ _____ _____   k. Teacher criticizes or punishes another student

30. _____ _____ _____   l. Teacher refuses or delays permission request

31. _____ _____ _____   m. Student appears to be bored

32. _____ _____ _____   n. Student appears to be searching

33. _____ _____ _____   o. Other (specify)

34. _____ _____ _____

35. _____ _____ _____

36. _____ _____ _____   Notes:

37. _____ _____ _____   _____

38. _____ _____ _____   _____

Data Collection (Part 1)

Record any information relevant to the following points.

Student's Emotional Response

1. Complains (he or she is disliked, picked on, left out, not getting share, unjustly blamed, ridiculed, asked to do what he or she can't do or what he or she has already done):

_____

_____

_____

Holt, Rinehart and Winston

2. Posturing behavior (threats, obscenities, challenging or denying teacher's authority):

_____

_____

_____

3. Defense mechanisms (silence, pouting, mocking politeness or agreement, appears ashamed or angry, talks back or laughs, says, "I don't care," rationalizes, blames others, tries to cajole or change subject):

_____

_____

_____

Check if Applicable

_____ 1. Teacher tends to overreact to student's misbehavior.

_____ 2. Student's misbehavior usually leads to affection or reward from the teacher.

_____ 3. Student usually acts out for no apparent reason.

_____ 4. Student usually acts out when idle or unable to do assignments.

_____ 5. Student usually acts out when distracted by another student.

_____ 6. Student usually acts out in response to the teacher's behavior.

Positive Behavior

1. Note the student's changes in behavior over time. When is he or she most attentive? What topics or situations seem to interest him or her?

_____

_____

2. What questions does he or she raise his or her hand to answer?

_____

_____

3. What work assignments does he or she diligently try to do well?

_____

_____

4. What activities does he or she select if given a choice?

_____

_____

Holt, Rinehart and Winston

Analysis

From the data you collected about this student, do you see any patterns that might lead to recommendations for the student's teachers if *you* were a counselor, as opposed to a prospective teacher? If so, please describe the patterns.

_____

_____

_____

_____

_____

_____

_____

_____

_____

_____

_____

_____

_____

_____

_____

_____

_____

_____

_____

_____

_____

_____

CLASSROOM MANAGEMENT OBSERVATION FORM D

Your Name: _____ Participating Teacher: _____

Date: _____ Grade/Subject: _____ School: _____

First Name of Observed Student: _____

Focus: Measuring individual students' academic engaged time by recording students' on-task and off-task behavior

Data Collection

Identify the student(s) whom you intend to observe before the observation day. Observe the first student on your list; if that student is absent, observe the second student on your list. Observe each student for thirty minutes during a lesson. At the end of each minute during the lesson, observe the student and mark the following activity that best describes the student's behavior. When finished, you will have recorded thirty observations. Put a check into the appropriate row to identify the observed activity. When the thirty-minute observation period is completed, add up the checks in each row, total the on-task and off-task behavior, and then work out the percentages for on-task and off-task behavior.

ON-TASK BEHAVIOR

The student is engaged in tasks related to academic material. These may include: listening to the teacher, asking questions, completing an assignment, and so on.

Record Checks Here

☐ = Total Number of Checks for On-Task Behavior

☐ = % On-Task Academic Behavior*

OFF-TASK BEHAVIOR

Record Checks Here

1. Daydreaming _____
2. Socializing _____
3. Doodling _____
4. Playing with other students _____
5. Misbehaving generally _____
6. Waiting for assistance _____
7. Sharpening pencil _____
8. Getting materials needed for lesson _____

---

*For example, if there were ten checks for on-task behavior and twenty checks for off-task behavior, the respective percentages would be 33 percent and 67 percent. Roughly speaking, one could say that this student had a 33 percent academic-engaged rate during this lesson.

9. Getting a drink of water _____

10. Leaving to go to the bathroom _____

11. Being interrupted or distracted from lesson by an intercom message, fire drill, another
     student, and so on _____

☐ = Total Number of Checks for Off-
     Task Behavior

☐ = % Off-Task Academic Behavior

Holt, Rinehart and Winston

Suggested Activity 4

CLASSROOM ARRANGEMENT

The working, teaching, and learning environments that teachers create for students vary greatly across grades and within grades. To gain insight into the physical as well as the instructional dimensions and implications of this range, complete one or more of the following tasks:

1. Gain permission to visit a large number of classrooms in a single school. Spend approximately ten to fifteen minutes in each classroom taking general notes about bulletin boards, file cabinets, chalkboard space, seating arrangement, aesthetic appeal, and so on. Spend the bulk of your time in the classroom just looking and trying to get a feel for the atmosphere and/or the learning climate.

2. After you have visited a large number of classrooms, compare and contrast three or more of the classrooms that you found to be interesting in terms of classroom design.

3. Arrange to observe a lesson in a room that you felt was well organized and tastefully arranged. Arrange to observe a lesson in a classroom that was poorly organized and less tastefully arranged. Use the lesson observation form from the Core Activity to collect data on the lessons. After data collection, compare and contrast the two lessons. Was there any relationship between the quality of classroom design and the quality of lesson design and implementation?

Suggested Activity 5

QUESTIONING

To help you gain a well-rounded view of the career that you are considering, we have encouraged you to observe as much teaching as possible because the act of planning and implementing lessons is a fundamental and pervasive dimension of teaching. In the same vein, we will now provide you with the opportunity to take a closer look at a significant component of lesson planning and lesson execution, namely the component that concerns question creation and questioning itself.

The development of patterns of questions that have appropriate variety, as well as of single questions that are intriguing and original, is a satisfying aspect of teaching. However, research has consistently demonstrated that many teachers deliver patterns or sets of questions that are predominantly lower order, that is, questions that deal with memorization and factual recall of information. These memory-level questions do not require students to do something challenging with the retrieved information (e.g., interpret, analyze, compare and contrast, synthesize, evaluate, create). Interestingly, some education writers have argued that effective teaching for certain groups of students will involve high percentages of factual, lower-order questions. At the same time, the wisdom of teaching (accumulated practical experience) indicates that most students benefit from judicious mixtures of higher-order and lower-order questions, as well as from the opportunity to develop and answer their own interesting questions.

The forms utilized in this activity will introduce you to a tool for determining the percentage of lower-order and higher-order questions asked by teacher and students in a selected lesson, as well as the teacher's questioning rate (the number of questions asked per minute). If you proceed into the final phases of a teacher preparation program, you will be able to utilize this tool to work out the ratio of higher- to lower-order questions in your own (tape-recorded) lessons.

The second observation in this activity will help you observe the effects of "teacher wait time" on the level of oral participation in selected classrooms and lessons. The research base on wait time dates back to the pioneering work of Mary Budd Rowe (1974). Rowe contended that slowing down the pace of question-and-answer classroom communication would have a variety of positive results. Recently conducted research supports this contention (Tobin, 1986; 1987). When students are given more time to think after a question is asked, more students are able to respond, the length of their remarks increases, and the students are more likely to listen and respond to each other. A good deal of research has shown that many teachers, after asking a question, wait less than a second before rephrasing the question, answering it themselves, or asking another question. Research also suggests that many teachers, for a variety of reasons, favor boys over girls when it comes to the opportunity to ask and answer questions across the curriculum and in specific content areas (Campbell, 1986; Sadker and Sadker, 1986; American Association of University Women, 1992). As noted earlier Teacher/Student Interaction Form 1 can be used to see if gender-defined patterns of behavior are manifested in the classes that you are observing. In addition, staff development efforts in this area have attempted to train teachers to expand their wait time to three or more seconds between the question and the next teacher move and also to eliminate gender bias. It will be interesting to see what results from your own observation in this area. Finally, you might find it illuminating to observe the style and pattern of questioning in a classroom without any predetermined focus to see where an open-minded, open-ended observation might lead. To facilitate this observation, we have included the Qualitative Questioning Observation Form.

HIGHER-ORDER/LOWER-ORDER QUESTIONING ANALYSIS FORM

Your Name: _____ Participating Teacher: _____

Date: _____ Grade/Subject: _____ School: _____

Focus: The ratio of lower-order to higher-order questions asked in specific lessons and the teacher's questioning rate

Information

Lower-order questions require memorization and recall of factual information. The student does not use the information in any way (to apply, analyze, evaluate, etc.). The student is asked to retrieve certain information from her memory bank.

    Examples of lower-order questions:

1. Who was the first president of the United States?
2. Which American president went into politics after a career in acting?
3. In which American city is the White House located?
4. Yesterday we discussed the factors that led to the Civil War. Who remembers which factor was considered to be most important?

Higher-order questions require students to use the information recalled in some manner—such as explaining its meaning, comparing or contrasting it to something else, making a generalization, applying it to solve a problem, or analyzing, synthesizing, or evaluating the information.

    Examples of higher-order questions and tasks:

1. What does this poem mean to you?
2. Do you think the poet embedded a special message in the poem? If so, what is it?
3. Why do you think Ronald Reagan was such a popular president?
4. Which generalization about the factors contributing to the Civil War appears most accurate to you? Explain your choice.
5. If you pull all of this information together, which solutions to the problem emerge?

Data Collection

Nature and Number of Teacher Questions

1. Select a typical thirty-minute segment of teacher-student interaction and tape record the teaching episode. Then enter on two sheets of paper the questions asked by the teacher and the questions asked by the students.
2. How many teacher questions were higher-order thought questions?
3. How many teacher questions were lower-order memory questions?
4. What was the percentage of higher-order questions asked by the teacher?

$$\frac{higher - order\ questions}{total\ questions} = percentage$$

5. What was the rate of question asking by the teacher?

$$\frac{total\ questions\ asked}{20\ minutes} = teacher\ questions\ per\ minute$$

6. How many of these student questions were higher-order thought questions?
7. How many of these questions were lower-order memory questions?

Holt, Rinehart and Winston

8. What was the percentage of higher-order questions asked by the students?

$$\frac{higher - order\ questions}{total\ questions} = percentage$$

9. What was the rate of question asking by all students? What was the average rate of question asking by a single student?

$$total\ student\ rate = \frac{total\ questions\ asked}{20\ minutes} = total\ student\ questions\ per\ minute$$

$$average\ student\ rate = \frac{total\ student\ questions\ per\ minute}{number\ of\ students\ in\ the\ class}$$

Analysis

1. Compare the questioning rates and questioning ratios (higher order to lower order) of teacher and students in this lesson. What observations derive from this comparison?

2. Analyze the content, clarity, and sequence of the teacher's questions. What observations derive from this analysis? Does this analysis lead to observations that are similar to or different than the observations derived from analysis of questioning rate and ratio?

3. If you were this teacher's coach or supervisor, would you have any advice to give about the questions in this lesson? If so, please spell out.

THE TEACHER'S QUESTIONS

1. _____
2. _____
3. _____
4. _____
5. _____
6. _____
7. _____
8. _____
9. _____
10. _____
11. _____
12. _____
13. _____
14. _____
15. _____
16. _____
17. _____
18. _____
19. _____
20. _____
21. _____
22. _____
23. _____
24. _____
25. _____

THE STUDENTS' QUESTIONS

1. _____

2. _____

3. _____

4. _____

5. _____

6. _____

7. _____

8. _____

9. _____

10. _____

11. _____

12. _____

13. _____

14. _____

15. _____

16. _____

17. _____

18. _____

19. _____

20. _____

WAIT TIME IN QUESTIONING ANALYSIS FORM

Your Name: _____   Participating Teacher: _____

Date: _____   Grade/Subject: _____   School: _____

Focus: Analysis of wait time in questioning

Information

Research has demonstrated that the number of seconds that a teacher waits after asking a question dramatically influences the range of student response in a classroom (the number of pupils who want to orally respond) and the length of individual oral responses. The wait time after the student's response is another influential variable, but in this activity we will focus on the teacher's wait time after he or she has asked a question. Parenthetically, a wait of three seconds is generally considered to be a productive amount of time, but some teachers find that their students benefit from lengthier wait times (five to ten seconds). Also, teachers often refer to this variable as *think time*.

Data Collection

Use a stopwatch and the audiotape of the teaching episode from the previous activity to answer the following questions:

1. What is the teacher's average wait time for lower-order questions?
2. What is the teacher's average wait time for higher-order questions?
3. What is the teacher's overall wait time for all questions?
4. Is the teacher's wait time for lower-order and higher-order questions generally consistent, or does he or she have a combination of very short (less than a second) and very long (five to fifteen seconds) wait times?
5. Do the students' responses appear to be affected by the teacher's wait time? If so, in what way(s)?

Analysis

1. What observations derive from your comparison of wait time for lower-order versus higher-order questions?

2. If you were this teacher's coach or supervisor, would you have any wait time advice to offer? If so, spell out the advice.

3. What other factors, beyond teacher wait time, do you think might cause a wide range of students to want to give an oral response?

QUALITATIVE QUESTIONING OBSERVATION FORM

Your Name: _____   Participating Teacher: _____

Date: _____   Grade/Subject: _____   School: _____

Special characteristics of class (class size, demographic profile, and so on):

_____

_____

Focus: None

Information and Directions

Much can be learned about the art of questioning simply by observing master teachers. Also, much that is pertinent regarding style in questioning does not lend itself to numerical treatment. As you observe master teachers, try to discern and to describe what makes their approach to questioning successful. Where possible, try to follow up your observation with an interview in which teachers have an opportunity to discuss their approach to question creation and delivery. Also, if you perceive a way to quantify your observations, by all means do so.

Holt, Rinehart and Winston

Suggested Activity 6

OBSERVATION OF COOPERATIVE LEARNING

As you progress through your teacher education program, you will have many opportunities to consider and discuss general approaches to teaching (direct, indirect, and self-directed), more specific approaches such as mastery learning, whole-language learning, and cooperative learning, and finally a wide variety of instructional strategies associated with one or more of the aforementioned approaches (lecture, discussion, role-playing, cross-age tutoring, sociodrama, sustained silent reading and writing, tableau, the seven-step "Hunter" model, bibliotherapy, and so on). Within this complex universe of approaches and strategies cooperative learning occupies a special niche and traverses a unique orbit. It is simultaneously an excellent instructional strategy, a highly effective tool for classroom management, and a powerful strategy for reducing prejudice and negative discrimination between boys and girls and various ethnocultural groups. Indeed, as Davidman and Davidman (1997, p. 87) note, "Research data accumulated over two decades strongly suggest that cooperative learning is a powerful cross-content, cross-grade level strategy for simultaneously accomplishing several of the goals of multicultural education, namely educational equity, intergroup understanding and harmony, and the establishment of positive, collaborative, empowering relationships between students, teachers, and parents." In an illuminating review of the literature Robert Slavin reinforces the preceding thesis with one caveat (1990). Although noting that there is ample evidence that cooperative methods are instructionally effective in grades two through nine, he observes that there are ". . . relatively few studies [that] examine grades ten through twelve" and that "more research is needed in this area" (1990, p. 53). Slavin concludes his research overview by noting that ". . . what we know already is more than enough to justify expanded use of cooperative learning as a routine and central feature of instruction" (1990, p. 54). Hopefully, we will soon see evidence that clarifies the value of cooperative learning methods in grades ten through twelve. We expect positive results; it would be strange, indeed, if a strategy that is so clearly helpful for eighth and ninth graders in the United States elsewhere suddenly became ineffective for students who are one year older. In any event, the key point for prospective K–9 teachers is that an extensive literature strongly suggests that they ought to become quite knowledgeable about this important approach to teaching and learning.

The Observation Task

With the help of your instructor, identify a teacher who is noted for his or her utilization of cooperative learning methods. Arrange to observe for more than one period or lesson, and where possible:

1. Arrange to observe in a classroom where the student population is characterized by ethnic and linguistic diversity.

2. Receive permission to talk with students after the cooperative group work is completed.

3. Try to interview the teacher about his or her approach to, and experience with, cooperative learning. For example: How long has the teacher been utilizing coop-

erative learning, and how did he or she get started? And has the teacher been influenced by one or more specific approaches to cooperative learning, such as those articulated by David and Roger Johnson, Elizabeth Cohen, Robert Slavin, Spencer Kagan, and/or Alfie Cohen?

COOPERATIVE LEARNING OBSERVATION FORM

Your Name: _____ Participating Teacher: _____

Date: _____ Grade/Subject: _____ School: _____

Special characteristics of class (class size, demographic profile, and so on):

_____

_____

Focus: The utilization of cooperative learning

Data Collection

1. Did this lesson have an instructional focus, and, if so, what do you think the teacher would identify as the main instructional objective(s)?

    (a) _____

    _____

    _____

    (b) _____

    _____

    _____

2. Was cooperative learning the main instructional strategy in this lesson or one of several employed? If the latter, which other strategies were employed?

    _____

    _____

    _____

3. Prior to releasing the students to work in their cooperative groups, what, if anything, did the teacher say to the students to promote effective functioning of groups?

    _____

    _____

    _____

4. What did the teacher do while the cooperative learning groups were functioning?

_____

_____

_____

5. Were the groups in this class during this learning activity in competition with each other? If so, what effect did this appear to have on the learning?

_____

_____

_____

6. Overall (across all groups in the class) how well did the students appear to be interacting with each other?

_____

_____

_____

7. In the one or two groups that you were closely observing:
   (a) How many of the students were consistently on-task in a (seemingly) productive manner?

   _____

   _____

   (b) Did students have the same or different responsibilities vis-à-vis the task, or a little bit of both?

   _____

   _____

8. Were the groups diversely structured in terms of gender and ethnicity?

_____

_____

9. In the group(s) that you closely observed did the member(s) of one cultural (girls/boys) group or ethnic (Hispanic, white, Asian, African American, etc.) group appear to dominate the interaction?

_____

_____

Holt, Rinehart and Winston

10. Did the students in each group appear to be playing special roles at least part of the time—expert instructor, encourager, scribe, reporter, praiser, resource distributor, time-keeper, and so forth?

_____

_____

_____

11. What did you learn about classroom management from observing these lessons?

_____

_____

_____

_____

12. From your observation of these lessons, what questions would you like to ask the class-room teacher?

_____

_____

_____

_____

_____

_____

Comparison, Contrast, and Analysis

1. What were the significant differences between this learning environment and other class-rooms you have recently observed?

   _____

   _____

   _____

   _____

2. Was the teacher's role (behavior) in this class different than in others you have recently observed? If "yes," please elaborate.

   _____

   _____

   _____

   _____

3. To the extent that you observed differences in student and teacher behavior in the cooperative learning environment, to what do you attribute these differences?

   _____

   _____

   _____

   _____

Suggested Activity 7
USES OF TECHNOLOGY IN INSTRUCTION

In the Core Activity we said that planning and teaching lessons comprise at least two-thirds of the real work of teaching. With this statement we wanted to remind prospective teachers that a lot of important teaching takes place between and after formal lessons as teachers engage in developing a variety of significant nondirective instructional activities and personal relationships with students. Such teaching will increasingly take place in learning environments filled with interactive technical devices (televisions, tape recorders, computers, modems, laser disks, and so on). The point here is that in the near future, teachers will increasingly deliver instruction via well-designed interactive electronic learning environments in addition to better designed individual lessons. For this reason, in Suggested Activity 7 we encourage you to observe teachers who carry on instruction in carefully designed technological learning environments. Although in many elementary and middle schools most students still visit one learning or computer lab for a specified number of minutes a day, during your career as a teacher, your classroom and workspace at school and home will increasingly take on characteristics of the computer lab that you will visit. In addition, it is conceivable that during your preservice and first years of teaching, you will join the thousands of K–12 and college instructors who are providing "classroom" content to past, current, and future teachers via their own Internet webpage. For this reason and others, we encourage you to observe and interview a teacher who is knowledgeable about creating effective electronic learning environments (ELEs). Examining a variety of websites would also be worthwhile, and the list that follows is but a small sample of the multitude of Web sites worthy of your perusal. Among other things, some of these websites will introduce you to interesting listserv discussion groups and instructions for subscribing to these groups. These Internet discussion groups will provide another vehicle and context for your analysis of teaching as a potential career. The following Web sites should prove interesting:

1. *http://www.ed.asu.edu/coe/*

   Professor Gene Glass of the University of Arizona reports that he and his wife in June 1996 compiled a large number of links to Internet resources where lesson plans are kept. You can use the preceding Web address plus a few mouse clicks (on "K–12 for teachers" and then on "Lesson plans"), or you can go to the lesson plans directly via http://www.ed.asu.edu/coe/links/lesson.html.

2. *http://curry.edschool.virginia.edu/go/multicultural/teachers.html*

   This is the address of the Multicultural Pavilion Teacher's Corner at the University of Virginia. This site provides resources for K–12 teachers of all subjects. It includes suggested reading lists, a multicultural activity of the month, students' music reviews, and links to other multicultural education sites.

3. *http://estrellita.com/"Karenm/bilingual.html*

   This is the address of Bilingual Education Resources on the NET, which provides links with multiple sites, including the Office of Bilingual Education within the U.S. Department of Education and classrooms across the country that are working primarily with Spanish-speaking children.

4. *http://www.caso.com/*

   This is the address of the Internet University, which is provided by Cape Software. It provides (as of April 1996) an annotated listing of over three hundred college distance learning courses available via the Internet. Course information is arranged by subject from arts to sociology. Information is provided about the institution offering the course, as well as tuition, fees, and contact information. A "Providers" section organizes information by college or university. A "Research" section provides links to mailing lists, FTP sites, usenet newsgroups, and telnet and Web sites with information about "on-line college and university study resources." In the future Cape Software plans an "Internet High School," with on-line high school and equivalency providers, and an "Internet Pilgrim," with on-line spiritual resources.

5. *http://www.csu.av/education/sitemenu.html*

   This is the address of Education Virtual Library. It lists education-related Web sites alphabetically and by education level, resources provided, country, and type of site.

6. *http://www.csun.edu/%7Ehcedu013/index/html*

   This is the address of a Web page created by Professor Marty Levine of California State University, Northridge. Professor Levine has compiled a page for social studies teachers. It points to lesson plans, resources, teaching strategies, current events sites, relevant usenet newsgroups, and other government, history, and Latino-related sites. The heart of the site is the lesson plan pointers page, with connections to hundreds of lesson plans in all areas and K–12 grade groupings.*

7. *http://www.ncbe.gwu.edu/majordomo/newsline/archive.html*

   This is the address of *Newsline*, a weekly newsletter of the National Clearinghouse for Bilingual Education (NCBE) at George Washington University. *Newsline* contains announcements and news from the U.S. Department of Education's Office of Bilingual Education and Minority Languages Affairs (OBEMLA), as well as grant information, job and conference announcements, and links to pertinent Internet resources, available via the Web and a mailing list.

8. *http://www.latimes.com*

   This is the address of the *Los Angeles Times* Internet edition, which debuted on April 8, 1996. It is scheduled to include daily news and features, coverage of movies and entertainment, a computers and technology section, a special section devoted to southern California sights and events, classified advertising, and chat boards. The site will be free. A fee-based site will also be available, with access to *Times* archives, as well as educational and research services.*

---

*The material in this annotation and in all other annotations followed by an asterisk comes from "The Scout Report," an on-line publication of Net Scout Services, which is an NSF-funded project within the University of Wisconsin's Computer Science Department. This material is copyrighted by Susan Calcari, but permission is granted to distribute verbatim copies of the "Scout Report" provided that the copyright notice and this paragraph are preserved on all copies. The InterNIC provides information about the Internet to the U.S. National Science Foundation: NCR-9218742. The government has certain rights in this material. Any options, findings, and conclusions or recommendations expressed in this publication are those of the author(s) and do not necessarily reflect the views of the University of Wisconsin-Madison, the National Science Foundation, AT&T, or Network Solutions, Inc.

Holt, Rinehart and Winston

9. *http://www.washingtonpost.com/*

This is the address of the *Washington Post's* home page. The site includes the full text of the daily edition, plus news from the fifty states, a daily congressional calendar, and over one thousand links to news, reference, and Web sites for over two hundred countries around the world. Features include movie reviews, book reviews (along with selected first chapters of books), links to over fifteen on-line comic strips, and sports features. A searchable archive of the previous two weeks' papers is available and, in the near future, an archive from 1986 to the present will be available. There are also several chat rooms on various subjects ranging from business to local Washington, D.C., issues. Although the *Post* is well known for international and national coverage, the on-line version is also very strong in local area news. At present, the *Post* Web site is completely free.*

Finally, for those of you already familiar with accessing listservs via your E-mail, several addresses related to multicultural education are provided in Chapter 10.

The Observation Task

On your own or with the help of your professor, identify a classroom, learning laboratory, or computer lab and arrange to observe instruction in this learning environment for several hours. Where possible:

1. Arrange to conduct your observation in a setting in which the instructor has a reputation for creative use of interactive technology (computers, videotape machines, television, etc.).
2. Observe different-age children learning in those technological learning environments.
3. Receive permission to talk with (interview) children about their learning during the class period.

Holt, Rinehart and Winston

TECHNOLOGY IN THE CLASSROOM OBSERVATION FORM

Your Name: _____ Participating Teacher: _____

Date: _____ Grade/Subject: _____ School: _____

Focus: The use of technology to deliver various forms of individualized instruction

Data Collection

1. What did the teacher do in this classroom or learning laboratory?

   (a) _____

   (b) _____

   (c) _____

   (d) _____

2. In what ways did the teacher interact with the students in this learning environment?

   _____

   _____

   _____

   _____

3. What things were students doing in this classroom as they interacted with technology?

   _____

   _____

   _____

   _____

4. What kinds of individual or group learning activities were students engaged in while you were observing them?

   _____

   _____

   _____

5. Did the classroom or learning laboratory that you were observing appear to have classroom management problems or discipline problems? If "yes," please describe them.

   _____

   _____

   _____

Holt, Rinehart and Winston

6. To what extent were the students in this classroom or learning laboratory engaged in the activity (on-task), as opposed to being off-task (in one way or another)?

_____

_____

_____

7. What were students learning in this classroom or learning environment?

_____

_____

_____

8. Were the students in this classroom or learning laboratory engaged in higher-level tasks (analyzing, interpreting, evaluating, creating, problem creating, problem solving)?

_____

_____

_____

Comparison, Contrast, and Analysis

1. What were the significant differences between this classroom or learning environment and other classrooms you have recently observed?

_____

_____

_____

_____

2. Were you excited by what you observed in this classroom or learning environment? If "yes," why? If "no," why not?

_____

_____

_____

_____

_____

3. Does the teacher's role appear to change in this kind of learning environment? If "yes," how are the role(s) of the teacher different in this case than in other classrooms you have recently observed?

_____

_____

_____

_____

_____

4. If students' learning behavior in this classroom or learning environment was different than that of students whom you observed in other types of classrooms, to what do you attribute this difference?

_____

_____

_____

_____

5. To what extent did the students in this classroom appear to be controlled by the technology, as opposed to being in a position to use the technology to have control over their learning process?

_____

_____

_____

_____

_____

6. To what extent, if any, did there appear to be gender or ethnocultural (African American, Hispanic American, etc.) group differences in the utilization of the electronic learning tools in the lab? If such differences are noted, what might be the contributing factors?

_____

_____

_____

Student Name: _____ Date: _____

Journal Entry

Inasmuch as this chapter attempted to put you into close contact with a set of significant day-to-day responsibilities of classroom teachers, your Journal Entry should concentrate on what you have learned about these important areas of classroom teaching. Specifically, your entry should focus on what you have learned about one or more of the following:

1. Lesson planning and lesson implementation in general
2. Lesson planning and implementation at different stages in a teacher's career
3. Classroom management
4. Classroom questioning
5. Student/teacher interaction and dialogue
6. Technology in the learning environment
7. Cooperative learning

Questions for Discussion

1. You have had the opportunity to observe many different lessons as a result of chapter activities. As you consider these lessons as a group, what characteristic of the lessons was memorable, intriguing, or surprising to you, and why was this the case?

2. Following through on selected activities in this chapter, you may have had the opportunity to observe teachers with varying levels of experience. What struck you as noteworthy about the comparative as well as individual performance of these teachers?

3. Did you find the observation of lessons taught by teachers with varying levels of experience to be a worthwhile task? If "yes," what did you learn that was helpful?

4. Most education researchers describe the American classroom as a complex place.

   (a) Did your observations of classroom interaction leave you with this impression?

   (b) If "yes," as a prospective teacher, how did you feel about this complexity?

   (c) If "no," what feelings were associated with your observations of classroom interaction?

5. The interaction between one teacher and twenty-five to thirty-five students in the context of a lesson is a special type of patterned interaction and communication, but it is not unlike the patterned interaction that occurs in several other organizational settings. What did the classroom interaction that you observed remind you of, if anything? In what ways was the classroom interaction similar to the interaction that you have observed or experienced in another setting? Does this similarity have any implications for your future career as a teacher? If "yes," please identify and discuss.

References

American Association of University Women. (1992). *How schools shortchange girls: The AAUW report*. West Haven, Conn.: NEA Professional Library. A summary of the report is available from the AAUW sales office (800-225-9998).

Brophy, J. E. (1983). Research on the self-fulfilling prophecy and teacher expectations. *Journal of Educational Psychology* 75 (5): 631–666.

Campbell, P. B. (1986). What's a nice girl like you doing in a math class? *Phi Delta Kappan* 67 (7): 516–519.

Davidman, L., and Davidman, P. (1997). *Teaching with a multicultural perspective: A practical guide* (2nd ed.). White Plains, N.Y.: Longman.

Good, T. L. (1987). Two decades of research on teacher expectations: Findings and future directions. *Journal of Teacher Education* 38 (4): 32–47.

Rist, R. C. (1987). Do teachers count in the lives of children? *Educational Researcher* 16 (19): 41–42.

Rowe, M. B. (1974). Wait-time and rewards as instructional variables, their influences on language, logic, and fate control. *Journal of Research in Science Teaching* 11 (2): 81–94.

Sadker, M., and Sadker, D. (1986). Sexism in the classroom: From grade school to graduate school. *Phi Delta Kappan* 67 (7): 512–515.

Slavin, R. E. (1990). Research on cooperative learning: Consensus and controversy. *Educational Leadership* 47 (4): 36–41.

Holt, Rinehart and Winston

Tobin, K. (Summer 1986). Effects of teacher wait time on discourse characteristics in math and language arts classrooms. *American Educational Research Journal* 23 (2): 191–200.

Tobin, K. (1987). The role of wait time in higher cognitive level learning. *Review of Educational Research* 57 (1): 69-95.

Wineburg, S. S. (1987). The self-fulfillment of the self-fulfilling prophecy. *Educational Researcher* 16 (9): 28-37.

Chapter 5

DEVELOPING INTERVIEWING SKILLS

This chapter is one of several in this text in which you will utilize interviewing skills. Although the focus will be on classroom teachers as a source of information, you will also have the opportunity to practice interviewing with classmates, student teachers, and college professors. Before placing you into the interview setting, we will provide you with specific information on how and whom to interview in K–12 settings.

It is worth noting that all of the interview tasks in this text are valuable because they have you, a prospective teacher, utilizing an exciting learning strategy to conduct teaching-related research right at the beginning of your career. These interview tasks will require you to be outgoing, articulate, well organized, patient, and a good listener. The time you put into them will be time well invested. You will see that your interviews will expand and modify the interpretations that you placed on various observed events. Many of you will be assigned to a teacher or will spend more time with a particular teacher during your early field experience; and through the interview process you may experience your first face-to-face professional exchange with a K–12 practitioner. With these interviews, you will begin your initiation into the rich dialogue about teaching that is occurring in many K–12 programs in this era of educational restructuring.

In this chapter we will focus on the structured interview and its most useful derivative, the semistructured interview. We choose this focus even though during the course of your teacher education program you will derive much useful information from the informal, spontaneous discussions you will have with teachers in a variety of settings. Although informal interviews definitely have their time and place, the semistructured interview is a particularly appropriate tool for prospective teachers who are trying to make contact with professional educators in the busy world that teachers inhabit. This will be even more true for the outstanding teachers whom we encourage you to seek out; in most cases they will have gotten their reputations because of the extra time and energy they put into their classrooms. This type of teacher will find it difficult to make time for a meandering, unfocused interview. You will also discover that the planned interview will work for you, first in helping to get you the interview and then in helping you derive the maximum amount of useful information in a short period of time, say, thirty to forty minutes. Let us now take a closer look at structured and semistructured interviews.

Holt, Rinehart and Winston

THE STRUCTURED INTERVIEW

The *structured* interview has several distinctive characteristics. For example, in a structured interview the questions will be written out in advance, and the phrasing and content of the questions will be checked to make sure that the questions are clear and easy to interpret. In addition, you will arrange the questions in a sequential, logical manner; will try to match the number of questions to the amount of time planned for the interview; and will write out a statement explaining the purpose of the interview. After the questions have been selected, tried out on friends, and put into their final form, write them on a notepad, with a page allocated for each question, to facilitate note taking during the interview.

When the questions have been identified, and when you know approximately how much time you will need for the interview and have carefully written out the purpose of the interview, you are ready to make phone contact with the teacher to arrange a time and a place for the interview. The first contact will likely be with a school secretary, and you should sound organized, polite, and appreciative as the secretary tries to find out when the teacher will have a break during the day. After contact has been made with the teacher, you should provide the teacher with (or indicate):

1. Your name and position within the specific teacher education program (are you a sophomore at Bowling Green University, a postbaccalaureate candidate about to enter the teacher education program, etc.?)
2. That you would like to arrange a twenty- or thirty-minute interview
3. The kinds of questions you intend to ask (two or three examples of your questions) and the purpose of the interview
4. The kind of flexibility you have for the interview ("I can show up at your school between noon and 2:00 P.M. on Mondays, Wednesdays, and Fridays")

Before discussing the actual questions that make up a structured interview, it should be understood that during the course of the interview it is natural and appropriate for the structured interview to be transformed into a semistructured one. This transformation occurs when you, the interviewer, choose to build on the answer to one question by asking a new, unplanned question. This is analogous to the situation that occurs every day in thousands of classrooms across the world when teachers diverge from their lesson plans to seize upon that uniquely fertile circumstance that educators commonly call the "teachable" moment. In the context of interviews carried out by novice interviewers, an apt label for the transition to the semistructured interview would be the "questionable" moment. Such divergence is extremely practical and highly recommended. The amount of time spent on the interview will likely be the same. Some planned questions may not get asked, but they can be included in your next interview. You will find that your interview will be more enjoyable and probably more revealing when you add questions to your planned structured interview, particularly if you follow the interview guidelines enumerated later in the chapter.

THE INTERVIEW QUESTIONS

The reader might well ask what comes first: the teacher or the interview? We recommend that you develop your interview first and then use your questions and inter-

Holt, Rinehart and Winston

view rationale to help you land your interview. However, it would be practical to think about the kind of teacher you want to interview as you develop your questions. For example, you might decide that your first interview will be with a kindergarten teacher as opposed to a sixth-grade teacher, or a junior high school science teacher as opposed to a high school English, speech, or history teacher. Focusing on a particular category of teacher will make it easier to generate grade-level-specific and course-content-specific questions; these are questions that would make sense only to a specific grade-level teacher or to a teacher of a specific course. Examples of tenth-grade biology questions are:

1. What kinds of laboratory experiences are a common part of the curriculum at this high school?
2. To what extent is the high school biology curriculum career-oriented?

After focusing on a particular type of teacher, the next logical step in the interview development process is to brainstorm and generate a randomly ordered set of questions. After the questions exist, the sequencing and refining process can begin. At this point the reader may be wondering: "Do I generate these questions all by myself?" Typically, the answer is "no." There are at least five sources of questions, and the five, in combination, will produce an abundant yield of appropriate questions. These sources are: the classrooms that you observe in, the professors in your teacher education program, your own curiosity, sample questions included in this text (see, for example, Table 5.1), and finally, questions shared by your fellow students.

To illustrate more clearly how a structured interview is developed, we are going to walk you through the development process in a step-by-step fashion. As we proceed, you will draw upon a set of general questions for structured interviews. These questions will include personal background questions that we suggest you use at the beginning of all, or most, teacher interviews.

THE STRUCTURED INTERVIEW DEVELOPMENT PROCESS

I. First, pick a category of teacher. For example, our category will be sixth-grade teacher.
II. Next, generate a list of questions.
   A. Select questions from Table 5.1. (For our example, 1, 2, 4, 7, 9, 10, 11, 12, 14, and 15.)
   B. Add other questions that stem from your observations in upper-grade elementary school classrooms, your own curiosity, and suggestions from your professors and fellow students. Questions such as the ones that follow will probably result:
      1. Why is it that, in several classes that I have observed, reading is taught in small groups and math in large groups?
      2. Why do you have the children seated in little clusters of fours with their desks facing each other?
      3. Is the sixth grade a unique or special grade to teach? And if so, what makes it special? In what ways is it different than the fifth grade?
      4. Do you have textbooks to help you teach all of the separate elementary school content areas?

In what ways are interviewing skills essential to effective communication between teachers and parents, students, and other teachers?

"Well, you see, Mrs. Smith, the reason your son is doing poorly in school is that he's dumb."

Used with permission of the cartoonist—Tom McCally
Holt, Rinehart and Winston

5. Does the school perceive some content areas to be more important than others? How does this attitude influence the actual delivery of the school curriculum?
6. How does teaching in the upper elementary grades differ from teaching in the lower grades?
7. When did you discover that you were going to be an upper elementary teacher?

III. Step 3 is the sequencing and refining step. We will arbitrarily select a fifteen-question limit for this structured interview. This means that we could select five of the questions just listed, integrate them with the ten questions from Table 5.1, and then work out a logical sequence. Here are fifteen questions listed in random order. Rearrange them to create your own logical sequence and then compare it with the sequential structured-interview schedule that we have created. Discuss any differences with fellow students and/or your instructor.

The Random List

1. Why is it that reading is taught in small groups in your class and math in large groups (based on prior observation in the teacher's class)?
2. What helped you decide to become a teacher, and what helped you choose to remain a teacher?

3. How do you think the role of teacher may change in the next five years?

4. Do you consider teaching to be a challenging profession, in the positive sense of the word? And, if so, what challenges have made teaching an interesting career for you?

5. How does teaching in the sixth grade differ from teaching in the first grade?

6. What have you found most satisfying in your teaching career?

7. What is the job like after school is out? Do you find yourself taking schoolwork home?

8. Do school administrators think that some content areas are more important than others? How do these beliefs influence the actual content and delivery of the school curriculum?

9. Before I ask you more specific questions about the teaching profession, could you tell me a bit about your background in teaching?

   (a) Years of experience?

   (b) Grade levels taught?

   (c) Numbers of years in this school? School district?

10. Do you belong to a teachers' organization, and if so, which one(s)?

    (a) How do these organizations help teachers?

    (b) Do they create any problems for the profession?

11. When did you discover that you were going to be an upper elementary teacher?

12. What important changes in the teaching profession have occurred during your teaching career?

13. Do you have textbooks to help you teach all of the separate elementary school content areas?

14. During your career, has teaching become a more interesting job? A more difficult job? What has made it more interesting or more difficult?

15. What advice would you give to a student considering a career in teaching in today's world?

TABLE 5–1
General Questions for Structured Interviews

1. Before I ask you more specific questions about the teaching profession, could you tell me a bit about your background as a teacher? (a) Years of experience? (b) Grade levels taught? (c) Numbers of years teaching at this school? In this school district?

2. What have you found most satisfying in your career in teaching?

3. What has been the most unsatisfying element in your teaching career?

4. In the positive sense of the word, do you consider teaching to be a challenging profession? And, if so, what challenges have made teaching an interesting career for you?

5. Do you consider teaching to be a profession? Why? Why not?

6. What do you do to keep yourself rejuvenated or enthusiastic about teaching?

7. Do you belong to a teachers' organization, and if "yes," which one(s)? (a) How do these organizations help teachers? (b) Is there a negative side to teachers' organizations?

8. If you were starting out all over and just about to begin a teacher education program, on which teaching skills or areas of knowledge would you place extra effort?

9. What important changes have occurred in the profession of teaching during your teaching career?

10. How do you think that the role of teacher may change in the next five to ten years?

11. During your career in teaching, has teaching become a more interesting job? A more difficult job? What has made it more interesting and/or more difficult?

12. What is the job like after school is out? Do you find yourself bringing home schoolwork after school or on weekends? On the average, how many hours per week do you put into your teaching?

13. Are computers and videotapes widely used in your school? In your classroom? If so, for what purpose?

14. Are there specific books, courses, or workshop experiences that have been particularly meaningful to you as a teacher? If so, could you briefly describe them?

15. What helped you decide to become a teacher, and what helped you choose to remain a teacher?

16. How did you end up teaching at your current grade level? If you had the opportunity to start all over again, would you obtain a credential to teach at another level, say, high school instead of elementary school?

17. What do you do that is particularly effective with students?

18. Would you recommend teaching as a career for your own children? Why? Why not?

19. What advice would you give to someone like me, someone who is at an early stage of the teacher training process?

Holt, Rinehart and Winston

The Sequenced Structured Interview Schedule

1. Before I ask you more specific questions about the teaching profession, could you tell me a bit about your background in teaching? (a) Years of experience? (b) Grade levels taught? (c) Number of years teaching at this school? In this school district?

2. What have you found most satisfying in your career in teaching?

3. Do you consider teaching to be a challenging profession, in the positive sense of the word? And, if so, what challenges have made teaching an interesting career for you?

4. What important changes in the teaching profession have occurred during your teaching career?

5. How do you think that the role of teacher may change in the next five to ten years?

6. During your career in teaching, has teaching become a more interesting job? A more difficult job? What has made it more interesting and/or more difficult?

7. What is the job like after school is out? Do you find yourself bringing home schoolwork after school or on weekends?

8. Do you belong to a teachers' organization, and if "yes," which one(s)? (a) How do these organizations help teachers? (b) Do they create any problems for the profession?

9. What helped you decide to become a teacher, and what helped you choose to remain a teacher?

10. How does teaching in the sixth grade differ from teaching in the first grade?

11. When did you discover that you were going to be an upper elementary teacher?

12. Do you have textbooks to help you teach all of the separate elementary school content areas?

13. Do school administrators think that some content areas are more important than others? How do these beliefs influence the actual content and delivery of the school curriculum?

14. Why is it that reading is taught in small groups in your class and math in large groups (based on prior observation in the teacher's class)?

15. What advice would you give to a student considering a career in teaching in today's world?

Now that you have your sequenced questions, you are ready to write down the purpose of your interview or what we shall call your *interview rationale*. When you make your first contact with the teacher, you will use this short statement to help you win your interview with a busy educator. Following is an example of an interview rationale for the listed sequence of questions. Please note that your statement should be direct and to the point.

INTERVIEW RATIONALE EXAMPLE

"My purpose in seeking this interview is to learn more about the teaching profession from people in the profession. I want to learn as much as I can about teaching as a possible career for myself."

Interview Guidelines

As in most complex endeavors, there are a few rules or guidelines in interviewing that, if followed, will help you have a positive experience. We will list some *do*s and *don't*s for interviewing. Here are the *do*s:

1. Be aware as you go out for your interviews that you represent your teacher education program as well as yourself.

2. Realize that both you and your teacher education program are striving to develop and maintain a positive reputation with the teachers in your region and therefore represent yourself and your program well.

3. Treat the data that you collect as semiconfidential information. You will share observations related to your data with your professors and fellow students, but you need not and should not use the teacher's name in these discussions. There is no instructional advantage in using such names, but there is the clear possibility that some misunderstanding may develop if teachers come to believe that they are being unprofessionally, and unethically, evaluated.

4. Be exceedingly polite and patient as you interact with your interviewee and other school personnel.

5. Dress professionally for your interview and in your particular region find out what that means.

6. Be better than punctual and come well organized and prepared to take notes.

7. On the day before the interview, call the school to leave a polite reminder about the interview. You can ask a school secretary to place a brief note in the teacher's mailbox: "Dear Mr./Ms. Smith, I am looking forward to our interview tomorrow and will meet you at your room as planned."

8. Conduct your interview in a private setting such as the teacher's classroom or the school library.

9. Follow up the interview with a brief thank-you note. You can write it in advance and drop it off in the teacher's mailbox as you leave the school.

Here are the *don't*s:

1. Don't bring a tape recorder to use or even ask to use a tape recorder on your first visit; our experience suggests that the pressure of the tape recorder, during the first meeting, makes the interview excessively formal.

2. Don't repeatedly interrupt your interviewee to comment on his or her comments; remember that you are there to hear his or her responses to your questions.

3. Don't interview your teacher in the teachers' lounge or any other public space in the school. (You run the risk of too many interruptions.)

4. Don't ask questions that could be perceived as rude, pushy, or offensive. Examples of such questions include:

   (a) "Do you get along with the principal of your school?" Or worse: "Do you like the principal of your school?"

   (b) "How much money does a teacher with your experience make?" (You can find this out at the school district office by asking for the district salary schedule.)

   (c) "Why does this school have such a drab environment?"

(d) "Doesn't the low status of the teaching profession bother you?"

(e) "All I see are older teachers in this school. Don't they hire young teachers in this district?"

(f) "The kids in this school really look messy. Does that affect their school work?"

Please note that questions 4a–4f ask about things that are natural for you to be curious about. But, on your first or second visit these questions would be unnatural and inappropriate for a relative stranger to ask. We mention the second visit because we have learned that structured interviews can easily lead to a follow-up observation and a second interview. When the interview has gone well, the interviewer simply says to the teacher: "You know, Mrs. Sanchez, I really enjoyed today's interview and learned quite a bit; do you think I could possibly spend some time observing in your class?" A semistructured interview would likely follow the observation.

At this point, you should be feeling more confident about carrying out a structured interview with a teacher. You have a clear idea about what a structured interview is, how to develop one, and how to use an interview rationale to get your interview. You have also learned about the concern that a teacher education program might have about its image and about your responsibilities to that program and to your own future. We will now discuss several other important interview-related questions:

1. How do you decide exactly whom to call for an interview?
2. After the interview has been arranged, how do you organize yourself for data collection and data analysis?
3. What do you do with the set of interview data that results from your several or more interviews?

Whom Do You Interview?

This fundamentally important question leads one to ask: "Why not go out and interview any teacher who is willing to be interviewed?" Indeed, there would be some wisdom in doing this. But there is too much variety in our profession to opt for this strategy. Our experience suggests that the teachers who can best help you decide whether teaching is the right career are teachers who have experienced success in their own careers. Thus, we recommend that the teachers whom you contact be ones who have been selected by the professors in your teacher education program or ones recommended by these selected teachers.

Collecting and Organizing Your Data

To collect data during and after your interview, we recommend that you employ the "key word-scribble-download" strategy. This strategy involves these steps:

1. Typing or handwriting your questions into an interview schedule and leaving three or four inches of space between each of the questions (the interview schedule is your sequenced, refined list of questions) and then making a photocopy of your schedule. Thus, you go into your interview with two copies of your interview schedule.

2. Using your first copy of the interview schedule to copy or scribble down key words or phrases from the teacher's responses for each question while maintaining ongoing eye contact with the teacher (a neat trick and something that you'll get better at).

3. Using your key words and phrases and your second copy of the interview schedule to write down your thoughts immediately or soon after (within an hour of) the interview. During this "download" phase, you will use your key words and memory to write up a more complete, extended description of the teacher's reply to each question. These extended descriptions provide the data for the analysis and synthesis described later.

4. Read what you have just written in Step 3 and, on the same or a separate sheet, list any new questions that stem from data in your notes.

Data Analysis and Synthesis

Data analysis is something that you should do for each individual interview as well as something that should occur when the notes from several interviews have accumulated.

To begin with, a day or two after each individual interview, you should examine your extended notes to see if you have anything to add to them. Occasionally, you will remember something forty-eight hours after the interview that was overlooked during the downloading, and sometimes you will see something new in your notes that leads to a new awareness about what your teacher meant by a certain remark. The examination might also suggest new questions for a second interview with the same teacher, or the questions might be used with a revised interview schedule for a new teacher.

At a later point, when you have the extended notes from several interviews, a different type of analysis will be appropriate. At that point, you will be in a position to compare, contrast, and make inferences based on the data that you have collected. After you have reread all of your interview notes and made mental notes of the points of similarity and contrast, it would be fruitful to answer the following question in your mind *and* on paper:

> From these interviews and (perhaps) follow-up observations, what have I (tentatively) learned or decided about teaching and the teaching profession?

Your written response to this question will be your data synthesis, and it will help you extract from the interview data the knowledge that will inform and influence your later observations, interviews, and decisions about a career in teaching. Some of these thoughts could be explored in greater depth in your journal notes.

ACTIVITIES FOR CHAPTER 5

Because the focus of this chapter was on the design and implementation of semi-structured interviews, all of the activities will involve you in that type of interview. The activities that we have selected, and their organization, assume two things: first, that some of you will be assigned to one main cooperating teacher during your early field experience and, second, that the interview with your assigned teacher will be most fruitful if carried out in the middle of the quarter or semester. At the same time, we encourage you to design and carry out brief semistructured interviews as soon as possible; your classmates, professors, student teachers in your program, and even your spouse can help you sharpen your interviewing skills (provided that you ask them the right questions).

Core Activity
THE SEMISTRUCTURED INTERVIEW

Design and conduct a semistructured interview with your cooperating teacher or a veteran teacher (eight to twenty-five years of experience). Use the key word-scribble-download strategy to develop a database from each interview. When the database is established, analyze your data to answer this question:

> From the actual interview, and from my analysis of the data generated by the interview, what have I learned about teaching and/or the teaching profession?

Suggested Activity 1
THE NEW TEACHER

Repeat the Core Activity; however, this time interview teachers who have been teaching for two to five years. After responding to the "What have I learned about teaching and/or the teaching profession?" question, compare and contrast the responses to the veteran and new teachers.

Suggested Activity 2
THE AWARD-WINNING TEACHER

Design and conduct a semistructured interview with an award-winning teacher, possibly the county or school district teacher of the year. This interview should be conducted by two members of your class in front of the whole class and could be videotaped by the instructor for later use.

Suggested Activity 3
THE COLLEGE INSTRUCTOR

Design and conduct a semistructured interview with your favorite college instructor. During your interview (and observation) of this instructor, try to identify and then to describe the elements of this instructor's teaching style that seem most significant to you. If you choose this activity, the following questions may prove helpful:

1. What characteristics or behaviors combine to make this instructor so successful?
2. What characteristics make this instructor a special, almost unique teacher?
3. Which aspects of this instructor's teaching style or behavioral performance appear to be artful in nature?

Holt, Rinehart and Winston

Suggested Activity 4

THE TYPICAL TEACHER'S DAY

Now that you've had the opportunity to orient yourself physically within the school building and the classroom, you will find it helpful to orient yourself to a typical day in the life of a teacher. Although most teachers would argue that none of their days is typical, careful observation and some well-stated questions should give you a reasonably clear picture of how your cooperating teacher spends his or her time.

The core of the teacher's daily activities will be the courses or content areas that he or she teaches. Using those as the cornerstones of your teacher's daily time grid, complete the grid that follows by questioning the teacher about the following:

1. What time does the teacher usually arrive at school?

2. What kinds of activities does the teacher engage in between arriving at school and the beginning of classes? Any special duties or regularly scheduled meetings?

3. How is the teacher's time spent between classes and/or during free periods, lunch, recess, and so on?

4. During class time, is the teacher constantly directing instruction, or are free times* built into the teaching schedule?

5. Ask the teacher to estimate the percentage of his or her daily time that is spent doing non-instructional activities (i.e., bus duty, lunchroom duty, administrative paperwork, calling parents, collecting money, checking attendance, etc.).

6. How much time does the teacher spend in the building after school? Is that by choice? What activities usually take up after-school time?

---

*Free times could be segments of time when students do seat-work and the teacher grades papers or handles routine administrative paperwork.

Holt, Rinehart and Winston

7. What extracurricular activities is the teacher in charge of? How much time does that take per day?

8. Ask the teacher to estimate the total number of hours that he or she spends per day in school-related activities.

THE TEACHER'S DAY

On the grid that follows, indicate the predominant activities during the teacher's waking hours. In the space provided, indicate the duration of the activity and whether it was school-related or nonschool-related time.

Description

Time of Activity	School Related	Nonschool Related
6:00 A.M.		
to		
7:00 A.M.		
to		
8:00 A.M.		
to		
9:00 A.M.		
to		
10:00 A.M.		
to		
11:00 A.M.		
to		
noon		
to		
1:00 P.M.		
to		
2:00 P.M.		
to		
3:00 P.M.		
to		
4:00 P.M.		
to		
5:00 P.M.		
to		
6:00 P.M.		
to		
7:00 P.M.		
to		
8:00 P.M.		
to		
9:00 P.M.		
to		
10:00 P.M.		
to		
11:00 P.M.		
to		
midnight		

Holt, Rinehart and Winston

TABULATE THE FOLLOWING:

1. Total number of hours in teacher's typical workday: _____

2. Percentage of time spent in school-related activities: _____%

3. Percentage of time spent in nonschool-related activities: _____%

4. Percentage of school-related activities that are noninstructional: _____%

5. Total number of hours spent teaching or performing instructionally related activities (setting up labs, learning centers, etc.): _____

Although the public's general impression is that teachers work from 8:30 A.M. to 3:30 P.M. and have June, July, and August for vacation time, nothing could be further from the truth. Teachers' days are usually long, and their schedules rarely allow much time for relaxing, regrouping, and regenerating. During the day, relaxation time consists mainly of stolen moments because even free periods are consumed with preparing for class, grading papers, or calling parents. In addition, the three months' summer vacation is often spent either taking additional graduate course work or supplementing the yearly income or, in some cases, both.

To appreciate fully the rigors of teaching, one must analyze the amount of time spent doing school-related activities and the physical and emotional effects of the intensive nature of the work. Introducing yourself to schools and teaching requires a thorough assessment of the environments in which teaching occurs and of the conditions under which teachers perform their daily teaching and nonteaching routines. Even a cursory analysis provides convincing evidence that a considerable gap exists between the public's general impressions and the realities of the teaching profession.

Student Name:_____ Date:_____

Journal Entry

Inasmuch as this chapter focused on interviewing classroom teachers, your Journal Entry should comment or elaborate on:

1. What have you learned from the set of interviews that you conducted?
2. What are your thoughts about interviewing as a research strategy? Was it a strategy that worked for you, or did you find it difficult to gather information in the face-to-face mode? What did you like about the interviewing process? What, if anything, would you do differently in your next interview?

_____

_____

_____

_____

_____

_____

_____

_____

_____

_____

_____

_____

_____

_____

_____

_____

_____

_____

_____

_____

_____

Questions for Discussion

1. For a variety of reasons, in the past as well as in the present, the teaching profession has had an extremely high turnover rate. When you consider your future in teaching, do you perceive yourself as someone who will become a veteran teacher?

2. In the next chapter, on "Images of the Teacher," it is noted that the public has not always viewed teaching and the teaching profession in a positive light. Given the data derived from the interviews in this chapter and the observations and interviews conducted in previous chapters, what is your view of the teaching profession? More specifically:

   (a) Do you consider teaching to be a profession? If "yes," why? If "no," why not?

   (b) Do you believe that teaching is a profession or career that you will find satisfying and in which you will be able to take pride? Why? Why not?

3. The teachers whom you interviewed had the opportunity to discuss changes that might occur in the role of teacher in the next five years. Comment on the responses made by the teachers, and then ask the instructor of your course the same question.

4. Where and how do you think interviewing might fit into your approach to teaching?

References

DeVito, J. A. (1986). *The interpersonal communication book.* New York: Harper & Row.

Gordon, R. (1980). *Interviewing: Strategy, techniques, and tactics.* Homewood, Ill.: Dorsey Press.

Kahn, R. L., and Cannell, C. F. (1982). *The dynamics of interviewing.* New York: John Wiley & Sons.

Seidman, I. E. (1991). *Interviewing as qualitative research: A guide for researchers in education and the social sciences.* New York: Teachers College Press.

Steil, L. K., Barker, L. L., and Watson, K. W. (1983). *Effective listening.* Reading, Mass.: Addison-Wesley.

Stewart, C. J., and Cash, W. B., Jr. (1988). *Interviewing: Principles and practices* (5th ed.). Dubuque, Iowa: William C. Brown.

Wilmot, W. W. (1987). *Dyadic communications.* New York: Random House/Alfred Knopf.

Holt, Rinehart and Winston

Chapter 6

IMAGES OF THE TEACHER

Up to this point you've been directing your observations and your thinking toward the school and the people who work in it. You've begun the process of examining what occurs in school buildings and classrooms and why some schools seem to be more successful than others in reaching their goals. Because your primary purpose is to discover if you want to become a teacher the role or image of the teacher in the school is of critical importance. The focus of this chapter is on the teacher, or rather on the image of the teacher, and how that image has affected your perception of the teaching profession. You may be surprised to discover that the image of teachers that you've come to accept is a result of both your own experience in schools and the depiction of teachers by others who influence you in conscious and unconscious ways.

Because of these influences, your *decision* to enter teaching will be shaped by this combination of experiences in school and by images of teachers presented in books, newspapers, movies, and television. Teachers, like doctors and lawyers, are often inviting targets for media stereotypes. However, doctors and lawyers, unlike teachers, are often presented as dedicated professionals employing considerable intelligence and/or occasional wit in solving the perplexing problems of their professions with the latest practices and technologies. Conversely, teachers are rarely shown doing more than handling "problem" students or dealing with unsympathetic administrators.* Although television viewers are frequently provided with insights into the courtroom practices of talented lawyers and the operating room techniques of skilled surgeons, teachers are usually depicted employing the most traditional methodologies (lectures/discussions) with students who are generally eager for periods of somewhere around five minutes. Not surprisingly, teaching usually looks easy under those conditions. Only recently have the media begun to portray teachers in realistic and more positive roles.

What of these images? To what extent do they influence our perceptions of teachers and teaching? How accurate are they? What impact have they had on those teachers currently in the profession? The answers to some of these questions, of

---

*Interestingly, principals are almost always portrayed as unsympathetic, autocratic pencil pushers thoroughly wrapped up in maintaining the bureaucracy at all costs. In that sense, they usually come off as looking worse than the teachers.

Holt, Rinehart and Winston

course, will lie within the context of your observations and interviews with teachers. Others, however, lie within you as you have had your perceptions molded and "massaged" by the media. In the next section, we'll explore how some of these images have been created by various media. Gauge your reaction to the degree to which these images influenced or did not influence you. Then pose some of these same questions to classroom teachers to determine how much they see of themselves and others in these images.

THE TEACHER IN LITERATURE, FILM, AND TELEVISION

From Washington Irving's characterization of Ichabod Crane as a hapless pedagogue immersed in his own self-importance and fears, to Mark Twain's depiction of the one-room schoolmaster who sneaks a peek at *Gray's Anatomy* and has his "dome gilded" (his bald head painted gold) by Tom Sawyer and his friends, to the more sympathetic, two-dimensional view of the young, but obviously misguided, progressive elementary teacher in Harper Lee's *To Kill a Mockingbird,* the treatment of teachers in literature has only occasionally been positive.

Female teachers in literature are often depicted as unattractive physically, undesirable sexually, and unskilled socially. The "schoolmarm" image remains the dominant perspective of many writers. Male teachers fare little better, although they are occasionally shown as having lustful yearnings for a two-dimensional female character. These yearnings, however, inevitably lead to the teacher's downfall in the community. The literary message is quite clear. Teachers are ordinary-looking, asexual, moderately intelligent (though often in an eccentric way), socially inept public servants. Their ambitions are minimal and limited primarily to salvaging some recalcitrant student(s). Females teach only until they can find a suitable mate or, because of a jilted love, until they become schoolmarmish spinsters. More recently, however, novels by Judy Blume and others have presented teachers in a realistic, positive light. These literary images may possibly have affected your perceptions of teaching.

Research on Hollywood films over the past fifty years suggests that teachers have fared as poorly in that medium as they have in literature. Teachers in films made prior to the 1970s are frequently shown as pedantic, dull, and sometimes cruel to their students. Even when teachers are depicted as sympathetic to the needs of adolescents, they are also shown as being confused by the actions of young people and dismayed by the differences in the basic values held by the students and themselves. It appears in numerous cases that the teachers have had little formal training in psychology, pedagogy, and philosophy and have literally stepped in front of the class with little more than the force of their personalities to get them through.

Even when teachers are depicted in a positive light in books and in films such as Sidney Poitier in *To Sir with Love,* Nick Nolte in *Teachers,* William Hurt in *Children of a Lesser God,* and Robin Williams in *Dead Poets Society,* they are shown struggling against enormous odds at great personal cost. Frequently, despite their best efforts, these teachers are defeated by "the system." Teachers, it appears, must either be social misfits, crusading missionaries, or superheroes. These are images that can create an unrealistic view of education and teaching, particularly when contrasted against the realities of classroom life in most schools. Rarely does one find a Mr.

Chips or a Miss Dove or a Miss Jean Brodie in elementary or secondary classrooms and schools. When portrayed as larger than life on film, characters like Mr. Chips have a way of blending with our actual experiences in schools to create a curious mixture of fantasy and reality in our unconscious. Because of the prolonged and frequently intense nature of our school experiences, as opposed to our limited experience with doctors and lawyers, film images can have a powerful effect on our recollection of teachers in a manner that is unlike our recollection of any other profession.

Television images have an impact on perceptions that frequently exceeds that of film. Films depict memorable people, whereas television depicts memorable characters. The image of the teacher, as depicted by television writers, has evolved in a curious manner over the past five decades. In the 1950s teachers were seen as comedic individuals who had to maintain their resolute calmness when faced with the light-hearted antics of their students (e.g., *Our Miss Brooks*). In the 1960s and early 1970s the serious-minded, student-centered teachers such as Mr. Novak or Pete Dixon (*Room 222*) appeared on the school scene to guide their frequently troubled charges through adolescence. Although sometimes humorous, these teachers were never comedic. No doubt, many of the teachers whom you had in school were influenced by some of these images as they made their decision to enter teaching. Indeed, during this period (1965–1975) more people entered teaching than during any other decade before or since.

The late 1970s ushered in the teacher as stand-up comedian when the Sweathogs welcomed back Kotter (Gabe Kaplan). Here, the teacher was totally immersed in the lives of his students, and they in his. This, of course, was because he had been "one of them," proving that in teaching, unlike many other professions, you *can* go home again. Although essentially a situation comedy and vehicle for Gabe Kaplan, this popular series portrayed the teacher as caring, clever, and, on the whole, serious and positive. Kotter's positive teacher image is in the same vein as the images of hard-working, intelligent teachers of *Room 222* and the generally positive images presented in the New York City–based television series, *Fame*. In the 1980s several comedy and dramatic series continued this positive trend. In *Head of the Class*, a nomadic substitute teacher was drawn into a class of gifted students. He was shown as student-centered, comic-serious, and thoroughly dedicated to his gifted "Sweathogs." In the *Bronx Zoo,* teachers, and particularly the principal, struggled against some enormous problems in order to make school a positive experience for students. As might be expected in any large high school, the teachers covered a range of attitudes, skills, and levels of dedication to the task.

In the 1990s the image of the teacher on television has begun to shift somewhat. Although medical shows such as *E. R.* and *Chicago Hope* show innovative medical techniques and the sometimes routine, sometimes hectic life of an emergency room, schools and classrooms tend to still be drawn from the same visual images that dominated in the 1950s. In the early 1990s *L.A. Law* and *Law and Order* showed how exciting and stimulating the legal profession could be, whereas recent police dramas such as *N.Y.P.D. Blue* and *Homicide* show the gritty side of being a detective in a major city. Whether in an emergency room, a court room, or a squad room, doctors, lawyers, and police officers are seen as having interesting and challenging professions.

Holt, Rinehart and Winston

Unfortunately, the same can't be said for classroom teachers. Neither their jobs nor the places where they work (classrooms) are shown with any depth of understanding. If teachers have interesting, exciting, or challenging lives, it is because of the *people* with whom they interact (students, parents, community members), not the *profession*. By the 1996–1997 television season, the teaching profession was the most frequently depicted profession on television. Unfortunately, it was also among the *worst*-depicted professions on television. As one critic noted, the 1960s and 1970s, television shows about school showed that "the teachers really wanted to teach, the students weren't smarter than the teacher, and you actually learned a thing or two." The critic went on to "grade" the new television programs about schools and noted that he "fears for our fictitious educational system." The highest-graded show (*Pearl*) is actually about a college classroom, so the remaining new shows (*Dangerous Minds, Mr. Rhodes, Nick Fresno: Licensed Teacher*, and *The Steve Harvey Show*) range somewhere between a *B* and a *D* on this critic's grading scale.

Again, although one could argue that the teaching profession is at least being noticed and highlighted, one wonders how much respect is being gained through this notice. Mercifully, many of these badly drawn images of teachers and teaching disappear after one or two seasons (e.g., *Drexel's Class, Parker Lewis*), but it is troubling that television producers and writers have spent so little effort to depict the teaching profession meaningfully, especially in comparison with the effort put into medical shows, lawyer shows, and police dramas that often feature recognized experts in those fields as either writers or consultants.

Although we have seen an uneven progression toward more serious, mature teachers in school-based books, movies, and television series in the past ten years, the images of teachers created by the media still leave much to be desired in terms of authenticity, depth, and variety. Because many adults grew up with the older, more distorted images of teachers and teaching, their perceptions of schools might be quite different than those of younger generations. Frequently, these more distorted images have found their way into the news media.

SCHOOLS, TEACHERS, AND NEWS IMAGES

In recent years, schools and the teaching profession have come under fire by the news media and politicians more than ever before. Much of this fire, of course, can be attributed to a general demystification of all institutions in American society that occurred in the 1960s and 1970s, but nonetheless, the criticisms have resulted in a serious erosion of the public image of teachers and teaching.

To what extent are these criticisms valid, and what effect have they had on teachers' self-images? Do these emerging images accurately depict the conditions of schools and the skills of teachers? To what degree do the following statements about teachers and teaching reflect reality? Why do local papers in small towns frequently present *positive* views of the schools in contrast to the views presented by the national news? Which view is more accurate? Why?

Holt, Rinehart and Winston

Core Activity

NEWS IMAGES OF EDUCATION

The following are some opinions that have appeared in the media. After each statement, indicate whether you believe that it is true or false, and give a reason for your choice.

1. Teaching attracts the less-capable college students. S.A.T. scores of education majors are among the lowest of any majors on college campuses.

   True   False

   Reason: _____

   _____

   _____

   _____

   _____

2. The teaching field has a distressingly high percentage of teachers who have difficulty writing intelligent sentences or even spelling simple words correctly.

   True   False

   Reason: _____

   _____

   _____

   _____

   _____

3. Drug usage is disproportionately high in elementary and secondary schools in the United States, rendering a positive, effective educational environment virtually nonexistent.

   True   False

   Reason: _____

   _____

   _____

   _____

   _____

4. The precipitous decline in family values over the past twenty years has left some students without any support systems at home to ensure the successful completion of their school careers.

   True   False

   Reason: _____

   _____

   _____

   _____

   _____

5. The curriculum in basic skill areas is so weak that the percentage of functionally illiterate graduates is increasing every year.

   True   False

   Reason: _____

   _____

   _____

   _____

   _____

6. Secondary teachers have reached a "compromise" with their students. In essence, teachers will lower their expectations and demands if students will behave in a reasonable manner.

   True   False

   Reason: _____

   _____

   _____

   _____

   _____

7. American students lag behind those of virtually every other industrialized nation in math and science achievement test scores even when our best students are compared with the best students of other countries.

   True   False

   Reason: _____

   _____

   _____

   _____

   _____

8. The number of private, parochial, and nonsectarian schools has risen dramatically nation-wide over the past ten years. The number of parents seeking to educate their children at home has increased simultaneously. Both increases reflect a growing dissatisfaction with the quality and focus of education in public schools.

True   False

Reason: _____

_____

_____

_____

_____

Are the teachers you are observing well respected by students, parents, and others?

"I would appreciate it very much if you wouldn't hum the tune from 'The Twilight Zone' every time I enter the classroom!"

Originally published in Phi Delta Kappan

The statements listed in the Core Activity reflect sentiments that have been given wide play in the news media and have created a negative public image of teachers and schools that is increasingly more difficult to overcome. As if to reinforce this negative image, the federal government established a set of National Education Goals, which were developed not by educators but by politicians. The National Education Goals and their supporting objectives have been widely criticized for being so ambitious as to be virtually impossible to attain by the year 2000. Thus, the argument goes, the federal government has set up the public schools for further failure and for continued criticism from the public when the goals go unmet by the end of the decade. Discuss the goals and objectives that follow to determine if: (a) they represent outcomes that schools should seek to attain, (b) they are overly ambitious given the current and predicted state of financial support for education in the United States, and (c) they reflect goals that educators would establish for themselves.

Goals 2000

Goal 1: READINESS FOR SCHOOL

By the year 2000, all children in America will start school ready to learn.

OBJECTIVES:

- All disadvantaged and disabled children will have access to high-quality and developmentally appropriate preschool programs that help prepare children for school.
- Every parent in America will be a child's first teacher and devote time each day to helping his or her preschool child learn; parents will have access to the training and support they need.
- Children will receive the nutrition and health care needed to arrive at school with healthy minds and bodies, and the number of low-birthweight babies will be significantly reduced through enhanced parental health systems.

GOAL 2: HIGH SCHOOL COMPLETION

By the year 2000, the high school graduation rate will increase to at least 90 percent.

OBJECTIVES:

- The nation must dramatically reduce its dropout rate, and 75 percent of those students who do drop out will successfully complete a high school degree or its equivalent.
- The gap in high school graduation rates between American students from minority backgrounds and their nonminority counterparts will be eliminated.

GOAL 3: STUDENT ACHIEVEMENT AND CITIZENSHIP

By the year 2000, American students will leave grades four, eight, and twelve having demonstrated competency in challenging subject matter including English, mathematics, science, history, and geography; and every school in America will ensure that all students learn to use their minds well so that they will be prepared for responsible citizenship, further learning, and productive employment in our modern economy.

OBJECTIVES:

- The academic performance of elementary and secondary students will increase significantly in every quartile, and the distribution of minority students in each level will more closely reflect the student population as a whole.
- The percentage of students who demonstrate the ability to reason, solve problems, apply knowledge, and write and communicate effectively will increase substantially.
- All students will be involved in activities that promise and demonstrate good citizenship, community service, and personal responsibility.
- The percentage of students who are competent in more than one language will substantially increase.
- All students will be knowledgeable about the diverse cultural heritage of this nation and about the world community.

GOAL 4: **SCIENCE AND MATHEMATICS**

By the year 2000, U.S. students will be first in the world in science and mathematics achievement.

OBJECTIVES:

- Math and science education will be strengthened throughout the system, especially in the early grades.
- The number of teachers with a substantive background in mathematics and science will increase by 50 percent.
- The number of U.S. undergraduate and graduate students, especially women and minorities, who complete degrees in mathematics, science, and engineering will increase significantly.

GOAL 5: **ADULT LITERACY AND LIFELONG LEARNING**

By the year 2000, every adult American will be literate and will possess the knowledge and skills necessary to compete in a global economy and to exercise the rights and responsibilities of citizenship.

OBJECTIVES:

- Every major American business will be involved in strengthening the connection between education and work.
- All workers will have the opportunity to acquire the knowledge and skills, from basic to highly technical, needed to adapt to emerging new technologies,

work methods, and markets through public and private educational, vocational, technical, workplace, or other programs.

- The number of quality programs, including those at libraries, that are designed to serve more effectively the needs of the growing number of part-time and midcareer students will increase substantially.

- The proportion of those qualified students, especially minorities, who enter college, who complete at least two years, and who complete their degree programs will increase substantially.

- The proportion of college graduates who demonstrate an advanced ability to think critically, communicate effectively, and solve problems will increase substantially.

GOAL 6: SAFE, DISCIPLINED, AND DRUG-FREE SCHOOLS

By the year 2000, every school in America will be free of drugs and violence and will offer a disciplined environment conducive to learning.

OBJECTIVES:

- Every school will implement a firm and fair policy on use, possession, and distribution of drugs and alcohol.

- Parents, businesses, and community organizations will work together to ensure that the schools are a safe haven for all children.

- Every school district will develop a comprehensive K–2 drug and alcohol prevention education program. Drug and alcohol curriculum should be taught as an integral part of health education. In addition, community-based teams should be organized to provide students and teachers with needed support.

By now you may have concluded that overall the teacher's image is rather shaky both within the profession and nationally. Although there is some validity to that conclusion, it doesn't mean that image equates with substance because there are more positives in the image than are generally recognized. Therefore, part of your growth as a teacher will involve confronting the issues of image versus substance, myth versus reality, and opinion versus fact. In the following activities you will explore the nature of teacher image and its effect on teaching and schools. From your explorations, draw conclusions supported by facts, realities, and substance.

This will enable you to discover that (a) society is deeply indebted to teachers and (b) many teachers feel very good about their decision to enter teaching. Along the way you may recollect a teacher whom you had who helped you out when you were upset or in a personal crisis. You may also find that teachers have many sources of joy as well as of frustration. Finally, you may learn that part of the challenge of becoming a teacher is learning to be yourself rather than fitting or overcoming an image that is neither accurate nor real.

Holt, Rinehart and Winston

Suggested Activity 1

MY MOST INFLUENTIAL TEACHER(S)

As you were directly experiencing teachers and schools during your childhood and adolescence, you were probably influenced considerably by your interactions with these teachers or with family friends who were (are) teachers. In addition, you were exposed to a variety of media models on television and in movies and books. These models also had an influence on your perceptions of teachers and teaching. In the spaces, describe the characteristics and behaviors (positive and negative) of these teachers and the media models that you were exposed to and briefly discuss how your perceptions of teachers and teaching were influenced. Please note that *your* influential teacher could be a media figure like Sidney Poitier (*To Sir with Love*) or Louanne Johnson (*Dangerous Minds*) or could be a real teacher whom you experienced in your own school career.

THE TEACHER(S) I WOULD MOST LIKE TO EMULATE

Characteristics:

Behaviors:

THE TEACHER(S) I WOULD *LEAST* LIKE TO EMULATE

Characteristics:

Behaviors:

Suggested Activity 2

MEDIA ROLE MODELS

Briefly discuss how your ideas about teaching are influenced by the teacher models listed.

1. Movie Roles:
   Male

   Female

2. Television Roles:
   Male

   Female

3. Literary Roles:
   Male

   Female

Suggested Activity 3

HOW DOES YOUR TEACHER FEEL ABOUT TEACHING?

In the previous activity, you were asked to examine your own images of teachers and teaching, some of which were derived from direct experiences and some from media models. In this activity, you will continue to apply your interviewing skills in a structured interview with the teacher whom you are observing and with other teachers with whom you may have contact. Besides the questions suggested next, feel free to incorporate some items of your own based upon your observations and class discussions.

1. Did any teachers whom you had in school influence your decision to enter teaching? In what ways did they influence you?

2. Did you seek to emulate any behaviors or characteristics of these teachers when you entered teaching? What are some examples of these behaviors or characteristics?

3. What do you perceive to be the public image of teachers in American society today? Is this image accurate or misleading? In what ways?

4. Do movies, TV, and novels depict teachers accurately or stereotypically?

5. Did you find any media role models of teachers to be particularly gratifying (for example, Sidney Poitier, Kotter, Mr. Chips, William Hurt, Robin Williams, Jaime Escalante)?

6. Did you find any media role models of teachers to be particularly disheartening (for example, the study hall supervisor in *Breakfast Club*, Ichabod Crane, Mr. Hand in *Fast Times at Ridgemont High*)?

7. How do the local newspapers contribute to your community's perception of local teachers? Do they portray teachers in a positive light?

8. Do you feel that you have to maintain one image in school and another image in your private life? Does that create any difficulties for you?

9. In what ways has the teacher's image changed since you began teaching? What are your feelings about those changes?

ADDITIONAL QUESTIONS:

From your data, what conclusions can you draw about teachers' perceptions of teacher image?

How do these perceptions compare with your own?

Student Name: _____ Date: _____

Journal Entry

Because this chapter concentrates on teacher image and how that image has evolved, your Journal Entry for this observation(s) should concentrate on your perceptions of teachers and teaching and how you arrived at your perceptions. Within this Journal Entry, you should elaborate on the feelings you had when you:

1. Interviewed teachers about their perceptions of teacher image
2. Considered the role that media play in shaping your and the public's image of teachers
3. Listened to your class members discuss their findings about recent criticisms of teachers and schools
4. Reflected on your own decision to enter teaching and the kind of public image that you would like to create as a teacher

_____

_____

_____

_____

_____

_____

_____

_____

_____

_____

_____

_____

_____

_____

_____

_____

_____

_____

_____

_____

Questions for Discussion

1. How critical is the public's image of teachers and teaching to your decision to enter teaching?

2. How could teachers improve their image with the public? Suggest some strategies that school districts, teachers' organizations, or student teacher groups might employ to attain this improvement.

3. Some critics have suggested that teachers create two images—one that reflects their public persona and one that reflects their private persona. Based on your observations, interviews, and class discussions analyze the extent to which teachers do create two distinct images.

4. Given your analyses of the media models of teachers, discuss how these models create stereotypes of the teaching profession and how they may create public expectations that are difficult for teachers to attain.

5. Describe your "ideal" teacher and the sources (real teachers, media models, etc.) that you drew upon to create this image.

References

Erndst, James. (October 6, 1996). Putting a grade on TV's 5 new school series. *The Toledo Blade, TV Week,* 3.

Feistritzer, E. C. (1985). *The condition of teaching: A state by state analysis.* Princeton, NJ: Princeton University Press (pp. 69-72, 92-95).

Husen, Torsten. (March 1983). Are standards in U.S. schools really lagging behind those in other countries? *Phi Delta Kappan,* 455-461.

Johnson, Simon S. (1987). *National assessment of educational progress.* Denver, Colo.: Education Commission of the States.

National Commission on Excellence in Education. (1983). *A nation at risk: The imperative for school reform.* Washington, D.C.

Sizer, T. (1984). *Horace's compromise: The dilemma of the American high school.* Boston: Houghton Mifflin.

Williams, D. A. (September 1985). Why teachers fail. *Newsweek,* 64-66.

Chapter 7

THE SCHOOL AND ITS COMMUNITY

Once upon a time, there were no schools. One learned everything from one's family or tribe or from the hard lessons of direct experience. Most of what was to be learned were survival skills: how to hunt, trap, keep the fire going, and find good water. Poor learners and slow learners usually had short lives, both individually and as communities. Experience was, indeed, a very harsh teacher.

As time progressed, some tribal communities developed more and more skills and had more and more to pass on to their young. Increasingly, too, it seemed inefficient for everyone to do everything. It became clear that people had different talents, different contributions to make to the welfare of the community. Some could build; some could hunt; some could lead. The human community discovered the specialization of labor. The accumulation of knowledge and skills, plus the specialization of labor, linked tightly to the history of education. At a certain point in the evolution of the human community it became inefficient for parents to spend so much time teaching their children. The education of Alexander the Great is a case in point. Alexander's father, Philip of Macedon, was too busy ruling and extending his empire to teach his son all he knew. But Alexander needed to know much in order to follow in his footsteps, so Philip hired the wisest man the world knew to teach his son. He hired Aristotle, and the great Greek philosopher became the personal tutor of the young man who was to conquer and rule all of the known world.

But as the example suggests, formal education was a luxury, something reserved for the elite. In the Roman Empire, wealthy families often had teachers who were captured slaves from far-off lands. Later the church opened schools, usually attached to monasteries. These often evolved into universities, where knowledge was collected, copied, codified, and passed on. Royal courts began to hire teachers. Later the wealthy merchant classes hired tutors, and they established small schools for their children. But in all of these examples, schooling was by and large something of a social luxury and reserved for those who would eventually lead the community in some way: as rulers, as churchmen, as merchants, or, in order to continue the line, as scholar-teachers. Schools, then, served the social elite of the community and, only indirectly, the rest.

Schooling was a major factor in the development of the New World. In colonial New England, Puritan parents believed it important for children to be able to read the Bible and, thus, to protect themselves from Satan. On the other hand, they were too busy eking out a living from the cold and rocky soil of New England to teach

134

Holt, Rinehart and Winston

their children themselves. They decided to establish schools and in 1647 passed the Old Deluder Act.* This historic act set the pattern for community-supported schools. It required that every town of fifty or more families pay a man to teach the children to read and write. From these beginnings, schools spread across and down the continent. As knowledge and skills developed and as the demands of commerce and an ever-more-complex business world emerged, schools snowballed in number. Instead of education being the province of the rulers and the wealthy, it was spread to everyone. More and more children began to go to school for longer and longer periods of time. Grades and levels of schooling were established. Grammar schools were followed by high schools.

Following the pattern set in New England, communities saw that it was in their best interest to aquire education. So education became compulsory, and it continued to require more and more time from the lives of children. Also, the specialization of labor that originally led to the selection of certain people to be teachers (to be, in effect, culture carriers) also led to increasing specialization among teachers. As communities wanted to be taught more and more, it became clear that specialization was needed *within* teaching. So the education of elementary teachers for the primary grades, physics teachers for the more advanced students, and so on, flourished. Even today it is a safe wager that both of these trends—toward more education for more people and more specialization within teaching—will increase.

Schools, then, have developed as a direct result of community needs and demands. As such, they reflect what a community believes it needs to survive. In times of rapid social and technological changes, like the present, schools represent what people think their children will need in order to live successful lives and to maintain the community in the future. And communities make very different choices. The Amish communities in the Midwest have rejected much of the twentieth century's technological progress and its values. As a result, Amish schools teach Bible and the basics and shun much of literature, science, mathematics, and the vocational programs that make up much of modern schools.

One of the most distinctive features of the American system of education is the relationship between schools and their communities. For one thing, we have a highly decentralized school system, which allows a local community to have an enormous range of choice in how it wishes to structure school and what it wants to teach its children. Most modern nations, like Russia and France, on the other hand, are quite centralized. How the minister of education in Moscow or Paris defines what will be taught in the third grade or in the eleventh grade will be taught throughout the country. The minister of education, in effect, provides all of the people one set of choices about what children will need. In our country, we have approximately sixteen thousand centers of education power: sixteen thousand school districts, sixteen thousand boards of education, sixteen thousand superintendents of schools. And, as opposed to Russia and France, which make only one social gamble about schooling, we make sixteen thousand different gambles.

The stakes of this educational wager are high, whether we are talking about neighboring communities in this nation or competing nations. Few communities are of one mind about what their future citizens will need; thus, decisions about the

---

*The act was so-named because the primary reason for establishing schools was to teach children to read the Bible, thus arming them against the snares and temptations of Satan, the "Old Deluder."

Holt, Rinehart and Winston

course of a school system are frequently heated with different groups wanting different kinds of programs. What finally gets taught is the result not only of the accumulation of knowledge and skills, but also of a political process, the struggle of a community over a classic education question, "What is most worth knowing?" Is it math and science? Is it how to get along with others? Is it critical thinking skills and the tools of learning? Is it character development and moral values? Or, how much of each of these priorities? Not long ago, Joseph Macekura, a junior high principal in Virginia, stated:

> A school is the child of the community—fathered and mothered by all of the dreams and hopes, and bred by the frustration and hopelessness, in the hearts of its citizens . . . society's expectations of a school is an ever-expanding one. Like an expanding ripple in a pond created by a tossed stone, each ripple in society envelops yet another demand for the school. Where chaos exists, schools are expected to create order. Where confusion and anger exist, schools are expected to calm group and individual upheavals and substitute hope. Where individual abuse and degradation leave their indelible scars, schools are expected to regenerate, like crayfish, a new appendage of healing and stability.

In a sense, then, schools are under pressure to be all things to all people, which is another way to say that they are frequently caught in the cross fire of a community's differing dreams and goals.

In general, though, schools tend to reflect the dominant values of their communities. In effect, we get what we pay for. But even in the best of situations, there are tensions between the school and its community. As noted, communities do not have one voice. Not only are there often competing goals, as suggested earlier, but also some people, such as those with no children or children out of school, may not be particularly interested in schools.

Another source of tension is related to the one just mentioned. Many people may have very different priorities for their tax dollars than schools, or "youth ghettoes," as they are sometimes called by nonsupporters. In the last two decades in this country we have seen a large swing in population and social priorities from school and youth development to medical insurance and the aged. Often those people with young children and those who have no children in schools are in conflict over how much should be spent on children.

A third source of tension is the relationship between what the schools are currently doing and what the community wants them to do. A school board member may voice a widespread concern for better writing on the part of students. But it may take several years to retrain, hire, and set in place a successful language arts program. Until the program begins reaping tangible results *and* the community notices those results, there will be strains. It is not uncommon, too, that by the time the school has reacted positively to the community's will, there are new board members with new priorities: One subject exits and another enters.

A fourth source of tension is between particular groups in the school community. Often parents with serious academic aspirations for their children may be at odds with what they perceive as the schools' "social adjustment" emphasis or their emphasis on sports. Sometimes working-class parents feel that the schools are giving too much attention to college preparation and not enough to noncollege-bound students. Differences may become so serious that the parents move and put their children into

How much of the quality of education in a community is a reflection of what the community values and supports politically?

"Aid to education sounds fine, but you and I know what will happen if the voters get too damned bright."

Holt, Rinehart and Winston

another public school or a private school. Generally, this is a luxury that only the rich and the middle class can afford. The poor are stuck with the schools in their community and rarely are able to move to search for better education.

A fifth source of tension exists naturally between parents and those who have a hand in raising their child. Teachers have a different function than parents. Teachers see the child in a different light, a more public light. Their focus is usually more narrow, dealing with a child's cognitive skills and social personality. They seldom see the private side of the child. They don't see the child embedded in a family network of events and aspirations. Teachers have only a slice of the child's life and lack the child's history, a history that the parents know intimately. Not long ago, the Boston-based columnist, Ellen Goodman, wrote about her feelings just as her daughter was graduating from the eighth grade. In her reflections, she lays bare some of the tensions that exist between the school and community members:

The mother had brought her daughter to this school with the usual baggage of mixed emotions. She signed the girl up for learning and turned over her hours and control. Her daughter was, largely, set on her own.

At times the two—parents and teachers, families and schools—formed an alliance. At times they had similar visions; at times quite opposite ones. But together they made a life.

From the first day to this, the last day, the mother had felt moments of uncertainty and distance from the school. On occasion she had overreacted, underreacted, misjudged events she hadn't witnessed.

At times, the girl must have felt as if she were in shared custody. She uttered lines that sounded like captions for missing pictures: "But that's what the teacher told me. All the kids are doing it. You don't understand."

After eight years, the mother was no longer surprised by any tension that existed between parents and schools.

Even the best of schools frame another world for our children, hurt them, reward them, test them by other standards. Even the best schools separate them from us, give them other adults, other rules, other ideas.*

On the other hand, neighboring communities in this country have very different educational systems. One community will tax itself quite heavily for its schools. The other won't, stressing instead recreation or programs for the elderly or letting people keep their money. One community will place an emphasis throughout its schools on math and science; another system on foreign language; yet another on physical education. At present, some communities are making a heavy investment in teaching computer literacy, whereas others are sticking to the "tried and true," concluding the notion that computers are a passing fancy. Said another way, what is taught in school is a social bet, a particular community's wager concerning what its children will need to live well in the future.

The relationship between a school and its community is very complicated. Although everyone wants children to have a good education, there are enormous differences of opinion about what constitutes a good education. Although everyone wants good schools, not everyone wants to pay for good schools. Although it may not appear so on the surface, public schools in the United States are heavily involved in the push-and-pull of the democratic process. Although school board elections are rarely involved in party politics (i.e., Republican or Democratic), they are political events in which the people directly elect those candidates whose educational views they find most compatible with their own.

Thomas "Tip" O'Neill, the former speaker of the House of Representatives, once commented on national politics by stating, "All politics is local politics." The elected public official who forgets this usually soon finds himself or herself unemployed. The same is true of school board members and the school superintendent—the person whom they choose to lead the schools on a day-to-day basis. They cannot get too far from the wishes of the community that they serve. This makes the American school quite accountable to its citizens, who not only elect the school policy makers—the board—but who also control the schools' purse strings by regularly deciding how much they are willing to tax themselves in order to pay for education.

---

*Boston Globe, 8 July, 1982.

We have mentioned that American schools are distinctive in their decentralized control. Elected local school boards and heavy dependence on local taxing are key to that decentralization. As opposed to countries with centralized control, with a minister of education making the decisions from the nation's capital, our schools are close to the people and quite accountable. They are also quite vulnerable to community discontent. One manifestation of this vulnerability is the high turnover rate among superintendents of schools.

We have emphasized the political nature of schools and the tensions that can exist in a community over schools in order to prepare you to look more critically at the school, the school system, and the community in which you are observing. To understand what goes on inside a school, it is often necessary to understand what goes on outside that school. It is important to know the community in which that school is embedded. To help you do this we have provided a number of activities and instruments.

Core Activity
YOUR SCHOOL/COMMUNITY IQ

Schools are a major part of a community. They are bound to their particular community by seen and unseen bonds, by past achievements and future hopes. Particularly in the United States, where schools are decentralized, the link between schools and community is strong. To know your school, you need to know your community. To know your community, you need to know your school.

The following exercise will enable you to test how much you know about a particular community and its schools. Do this exercise on either your home schools and their community or on the school and community in which you are currently observing. If you are in doubt about which to do, check with your instructor.

This test will confront you with issues that you may never have considered or for which you do not have answers. Where you do not have a ready answer, try to think it through. Where you do not have exact information, make an educated guess.

Holt, Rinehart and Winston

Student Name: _____ Date: _____

THE COMMUNITY

1. If an interested friend asked you to describe this community, what are some of the things that you would tell him or her? Like a good reporter, try to be as detailed as possible in your answer.

_____

_____

_____

_____

_____

_____

_____

_____

_____

_____

_____

_____

_____

_____

_____

_____

_____

_____

_____

_____

_____

_____

_____

_____

2. What is the population (approximately) of your community? _____ people

3. How large is your community? _____ miles wide; _____ miles long

4. What are the major sources of income of the people in your community?

   (a)

   (b)

   (c)

   (d)

   (e)

   (f)

5. Estimate the percentage of the working population in each of the following occupational groups:

   _____% Type 1—small business owner

   _____% Type 2—skilled worker (secretary, nurse's aide, technician, etc.)

   _____% Type 3—professional (doctor, lawyer, architect)

   _____% Type 4—public servant (politician, government worker)

   _____% Type 5—teacher or involved in education

   _____% Type 6—laborer (factory worker)

   _____% Type 7—tradesperson (plumber, carpenter, machinist)

   _____% Type 8—business executive, management, salesperson

   _____% Type 9—farmer

   _____% Type 10—homemaker

   _____% Type 11—other (specify) _____

6. What percentage of the adult women work outside of the home? _____ %

7. What is your estimate of the major religious groups in your community?

   _____% Protestant

   _____% Catholic

   _____% Jewish

   _____% Other (specify) _____

8. List the percentage of each of these groups in your community.

_____% White Americans

_____% Black Americans

_____% Asian Americans

_____% Hispanic Americans

_____% Other (specify) _____

9. List and estimate the percentage of the major ethnic and/or national groups in your community.

% _____

% _____

% _____

% _____

% _____

10. How would you describe the current state of your community? As a vital, **growing** community? As an old, but still vital, community? As a slowly decaying community? Describe in your own words what you believe to be the health of your community.

_____

_____

_____

_____

_____

_____

_____

_____

11. What percentage of people in your community are "newcomers"? _____ % Do people in this community refer to "newcomers" as "outsiders"? _____ What percentage of the people in the community would you estimate have attended the local schools? _____ %

12. In your judgment, is your community a good place for young people to grow up? Why or why not?

_____

_____

_____

_____

_____

_____

_____

13. Visit a police station and ask the desk sergeant to describe the crime situation in the community (i.e., major crimes, most frequent crimes). Ask in particular about youth crimes (i.e., most frequent) and specifically about drug use, underage drinking, and gang activities.

_____

_____

_____

_____

_____

_____

_____

_____

_____

14. Thinking broadly about the education in your community, list the educational institutions where learning goes on. Do not confine yourself to the public and private schools.

(a)

(b)

(c)

(d)

(e)

(f)

(g)

(h)

(i)

(j)

(k)

(l)

(m)

(n)

(o)

(p)

(q)

(r)

(s)

(t)

Is there competition among any of these institutions? If so, how would you describe it?

Holt, Rinehart and Winston

YOUR SCHOOL

1. In general, do you believe that teachers in your community are respected? Why or why not?

2. Where do the teachers reside in the community?

   _____% live in the community.

   _____% live outside the community.

3. What percentage of teachers attended the local elementary and secondary schools when they were young? _____ %

4. On the average, do teachers make as much money as the majority of people in the community? _____

5. How would you describe the relationship between the teachers whom you know well and the people in the community?

6. What evidence do you see of teachers drawing upon the resources, both personal and institutional, of the community?

7. Summarize your views on the relationships among the school, the teachers, and the community.

Holt, Rinehart and Winston

8. How would you describe your own attitudes toward this community? Is it a place where you would like to teach? Is it a place where you would like to live?

Note: If you had trouble filling out this school/community questionnaire, you may wish to get some help. The city hall or town hall is often a good source of general information about a community. So, too, are the local newspapers and the chamber of commerce. Because it is important for school administrators to know their community, they often have at their fingertips much of the kind of information requested here. Finally, the teachers and administrators in the school in which you are observing may be another source of information and insight to help you answer these questions.

Holt, Rinehart and Winston

Student Name: _____   Date _____

Suggested Activity 1

COMMUNITY MEMBER INTERVIEW

In this activity get the views of three community members (ideally, one should be a school board member) on the following questions.

1. How would you describe the community's support for its schools?
   Community member 1:

   Community member 2:

   Community member 3:

2. How would you describe the community's willingness to pay for good schools?
   Community member 1:

   Community member 2:

   Community member 3:

3. What aspects of a school tend to be most heavily supported, or what is most favorably viewed by the community?
   Community member 1:

   Community member 2:

   Community member 3:

4. What are the strongest criticisms that are heard about the schools from community members?

Community member 1:

Community member 2:

Community member 3:

Holt, Rinehart and Winston

Student Name: _____ Date: _____

Suggested Activity 2
EDUCATOR INTERVIEW

Pick three educators (ideally, an experienced teacher, a new teacher, and an administrator) from the school in which you are observing and, ask them the following questions.

1. How would you describe the community's support for its schools?
   Educator 1:

   Educator 2:

   Educator 3:

2. How would you describe the community's willingness to pay for good schools?
   Educator 1:

Educator 2:

Educator 3:

3. What aspects of a school tend to be most heavily supported, or what is most favorably viewed by the community?
Educator 1:

Educator 2:

Educator 3:

4. What are the strongest criticisms heard about the schools from community members?
   Educator 1:

   Educator 2:

   Educator 3:

Student Name: _____ Date: _____

Suggested Activity 3

TRUTH OR EXAGGERATION?

Social conditions change, schools change. What a community expects or demands of its schools shifts with new social priorities. Ten years ago a group of educators in Ohio wrote the following mock job opening announcement. The job description tells a lot about the realities of teaching but also exaggerates a great deal.

As you read through "Personnel Wanted" underline what you feel are exaggerations, and put checkmarks next to the more realistic points.

PERSONNEL WANTED

Openings are available in a variety of areas for special people. Are you in a rut? No variety in your present position? Are you a professional-type person who loves children and a challenge? Check the following requirements, and see if you qualify.

QUALIFICATIONS

At least a bachelor's degree (with an average of two additional years of college work).

You should also be . . . loving . . . arts/craftsy . . . athletic . . . resourceful . . . understanding . . . creative . . . loyal . . . enthusiastic . . . organized . . . dependable . . . knowledgeable . . . responsible to leadership . . . aware of fads . . . committed . . . able to update antiquated materials . . . accountable . . . fair disciplinarian . . . unfailingly cheerful . . . well-read . . . respectful . . . alert . . . quick decision maker . . . willing volunteer . . . multitalented . . . wise . . . charismatic . . . psychic . . . trivia expert . . . mechanically inclined . . . able to please everyone all of the time . . . honest . . . strong in nerves . . . sensitive . . . tactful . . . mentally and physically healthy . . . diplomatic . . . fair . . . diverse interests . . . well-informed . . . patient . . . attractive . . . unflappable . . . superhuman in stamina . . . not easily frustrated . . . able to enunciate . . . physically strong . . . community oriented . . . able to function in crisis situations . . . ABLE TO TEACH!

FURTHER REQUIREMENTS

You must be able to . . .

keep records . . . collect money . . . coach . . . support school functions (monetarily) . . . plan a curriculum . . . write behavioral objectives . . . write lesson plans . . . write reports of all kinds . . . attend seminars, athletic events, plays, carnivals, festivals, musicals, fund-raising events, parent-teacher organization meetings, graduations, committee meetings, school board meetings, department meetings, faculty meetings.

And be able to . . .

supervise lunchroom, recess, halls, bathrooms, study hall, detention, assemblies, plays, student council . . . prepare infallible testing instruments, create the perfect testing environment . . . evaluate all work . . . provide guidance . . . break up fights . . . check students for drugs and/or alcohol . . . deal with discipline . . . maintain a quiet classroom . . . interpret medical records.

Holt, Rinehart and Winston

Must be a(n) . . .

secretary . . . advisor . . . photographer . . . ticket-taker . . . librarian . . . curriculum developer . . . veterinarian . . . plumber . . . mechanic . . . biologist . . . handwriting expert . . . typist . . . interior decorator . . . entertainer . . . lecturer . . . janitor . . . carpenter . . . electrician . . . diagnostician . . . chauffeur . . . chaperone . . . nurse . . . statistician . . . dishwasher . . . housekeeper . . . psychiatrist . . . confidant . . . leader . . . cook . . . host/hostess . . . mathematician . . . historian . . . nutritionist . . . politician . . . accountant . . . linguist . . . cryptologist . . . author . . . companion . . . friend . . . file clerk . . . office machines expert . . . tear-dryer . . . hand-holder . . . back-patter . . . shoulder-lender . . . ego-builder . . . shoe-tier . . . nose-wiper . . . boot-tugger . . . clothes-zipper . . . lost book-finder . . . problem-solver . . . father/mother confessor . . . lovelorn advisor.

WORKING CONDITIONS

one book, chair, and desk you may have to share (the desk doesn't lock)

poor lighting, heating, and circulation

inadequate restroom and medical facilities

infrequent or nonexistent breaks with the exception of lunch and calls of a personal nature

institutional food (if you have the time and/or appetite)

FRINGE BENEFITS

all the gum you can scrape off the bottoms of desks

a growing collection of broken pencils, confiscated squirt guns, and miscellaneous animals, insects, and reptiles

vocabulary development (you will learn many new words)

exposure to original graffiti and love letters

more free advice than you can use

opportunity to move from assignment to assignment; from class to class; from school to school

high esteem in your community

exposure to various pathogens

If you feel you have the qualifications, if you love a challenge, contact your local school board office for an application.

Holt, Rinehart and Winston

Student Name: _____   Date: _____

Journal Entry

Your observation and study of your current school should focus on the relationship between the school and the community that it is serving and by which it is being supported. In this Journal Entry consider a few of the following questions and issues:

1. What tensions exist between the school and the community?
2. What attitudes toward this community's children have you detected from residents and from teachers?
3. To what degree are the teachers "of the community?" Are they similar, socially and educationally, to the majority of the parents whose children they teach? Do they live there? Do they reflect the values of the community?
4. What aspects of the school program (sports, dramatics, vocational programs, foreign language programs) receive a good deal of support from the community?
5. What evidence is there that the community financially supports the school? What is the physical condition of the school? Does the school have an adequate gym? Auditorium? Library? Computer labs? How does the teacher salary scale compare with that of communities around it?

_____

_____

_____

_____

_____

_____

_____

_____

_____

_____

_____

_____

_____

_____

_____

_____

Questions for Discussion

1. If schools were to disappear, along with the very idea of schooling, what other ways might we invent to prepare the young for adulthood?

2. How would the life of your family be changed if its members were responsible for the bulk of your education? What would be gained, and what would be lost?

3. Selecting either the school/community in which you are currently observing or your "home" school/community (the one that you know best), discuss the major tensions that exist between the school and the community.

4. What are some things that teachers, administrators, and students can do to strengthen the bonds between students and their communities?

Holt, Rinehart and Winston

Chapter 8

HUMOR IN THE CLASSROOM

Are classrooms a rich source for identifying humorous incidents? Do teachers who often use humor appear to be more effective than those who don't? Do students at different ages view humor differently? Are there gender differences that impact on the effective use of humor in the classroom? Does the use of humor increase student retention and achievement? Is it possible to "plan" humor into lessons? These questions, among many others, have been posed by researchers seeking to determine if humor has a place in schools.

Research on humor in teaching has emerged only recently. Most of the research has occurred during the past twenty-five years and has yielded mixed results (Neulip, 1991). Much of the empirical research has been done with college-age students, and the conclusions have only marginal applications to teaching strategies at the elementary and secondary level. Because of concerns over reducing test anxiety, a number of studies looked at the use of humor in creating test items for a variety of objective tests (multiple choice, true-false, matching, etc.) (Vance, 1987; Ziv, 1988). In general, research studies on application-oriented discussions of humor in the classroom stress the need to use humor judiciously, occasionally, and in a developmentally appropriate manner with a concerted effort to make it as relevant as possible to the topic at hand (McGhee, 1971; Gorham and Christophel, 1990).

Trying to analyze humor to determine what makes people laugh usually results in mixed reactions from readers. Part of this is due to the fact that humor is frequently derived from situational variables that are uniquely funny (i.e., "you had to be there"). It also assumes that the reader has developed the appropriate mental set to understand the humor (i.e., "I don't get it"). Finally, what the humor analyst believes to be screamingly funny is simply lost on the reader who has different tastes (i.e., "I don't like puns, slapstick, off-color jokes, visual humor," etc.). In trying to provide examples to illustrate types of humor that occur in classrooms, or in trying to describe how teachers can use humor effectively, any or all of the conditions just identified could come into play. However, that shouldn't dissuade you from trying to identify humorous aspects of teaching, working with students, or life in the classroom. Your success in making these identifications is largely related to how well you understand the development of humor in learners as well as in yourself.

At different ages and/or levels of cognitive development, learners show distinct preferences for certain types of humor. In the early grades (K–3), children enjoy conceptual incongruity (Burt and Sugawara, 1988) (e.g., "it's raining meatballs") and the simple absurdities of riddles, knock-knock jokes, and puns (e.g., "it's raining cats and dogs," "I know, I just stepped in a poodle!"). Older elementary (grades 4 to 6) children find physical humor funny and will frequently laugh when a classmate or an adult experiences physical discomfiture. By middle/junior high school (grades 7 to 9), humor frequently displays cruelty toward peers, diminution of adult authority, or "dirty" jokes. By high school, students' senses of humor become more sophisticated and usually correlates with what the teacher finds funny. In citing Gessell, Ilg, and Ames, Nikki Barnhart (1988) summarizes this developmental scheme nicely:

> Pure nonsense is enjoyed at an early stage of humor development, but children between the ages of six and eight would rather participate in humor that is understandable to them. By second grade children can create humor by word play, and some link has been found between cognitive maturity and the comprehension of riddles. Eight-year-olds have a strong humor sense and particularly enjoy stories where one person is fooled by another. By the age of ten, children enjoy slapstick humor as well as practical jokes, puns, and riddles. Twelve-year-olds like practical jokes and teasing as well as corny and smutty jokes. By thirteen, sarcasm begins and in another year humor is used against parents and authority figures. At fifteen, children begin to be able to laugh at themselves and then participate in adult-type humor at sixteen.

Reinforcing this description, McGhee (1971) described the results of studies done in the 1930s and 1940s with students in grades two through twelve. These studies found that students in grades seven, nine, and twelve expressed preference (most to least) for (a) absurdity, (b) slapstick, (c) satire, and (d) whimsy. Further, children aged seven to twelve found visual humor to be most preferable, with little or no appreciation of verbal wit. Children aged eleven to thirteen thought that situations involving someone's discomfiture to be most humorous, whereas fourteen- to eighteen-year-olds were characterized by their noticeable individual differences in sense of humor, greater appreciation of verbal wit, and their reliance on what in a particular situation was funny (McGhee, 1971). Although students today are more sophisticated in their humor and are exposed to a wider variety of humor at an earlier age, the predominant characteristics of humor at each stage are remarkably similar between today's students and their counterparts fifty or sixty years ago.

Although there are individual differences in preferences for various types of humor, most learners perceive a sense of humor to be essential to effective teaching (Korobkin, 1988). As mentioned earlier, however, what constitutes a sense of humor varies widely, depending upon the gender of the teacher, the age and developmental level of the learners, the subject being taught, the particular characteristics of the classroom situation and, of course, the personality of the teacher. Suffice to say that some teachers use humor with extraordinary effectiveness, whereas others are ill served by their awkward attempts to make students laugh.

Much of your development as a teacher will involve self-discovery and the ability to identify your strengths and weaknesses in working with learners. You may find that the jokes, stories, quips, and puns that your friends and family laugh at until they cry fall flat when you try them on students. Conversely, you may find the humor that causes your students to collapse into paroxysms of laughter to be incredibly unsophisticated and/or just plain silly. It is unlikely that you will walk into a classroom and become an immediate comedic hit with your first lesson. Indeed, it would be unwise for you to try. Rather, you should be concerned with becoming an observer of humor and a discriminating analyst of humorous situations. You should know when humor is appropriate and when it is distracting, embarrassing, or offensive. You should identify when learning can be enhanced through the use of relevant, insightful forms of humor. Finally, you should be aware that students don't expect their teachers to be stand-up comedians, nor do they perceive it to be particularly attractive whenever their teachers try to be funny in situations that do not call for it.

CLASSIFYING HUMOR IN THE CLASSROOM

In 1991 James Neulip employed an inductive approach to analyze and categorize high school teachers' use of humor in their teaching. Working from a series of studies (Gorham and Christophel, 1990; Nussbaum et al., 1985; Bryant et al., 1979) done with college students, Neulip expanded upon what he considered to be the limitations of those studies and created a taxonomic approach for classifying high school teachers' humor. This taxonomy contained twenty items organized into five categories: (a) teacher-targeted humor, (b) student-targeted humor, (c) untargeted humor, (d) external source humor, and (e) nonverbal humor (Neulip, 1991).

Teacher-targeted humor involves personal anecdotes disclosed by the teacher that are either related or unrelated to the content or involve some personally embarrassing incident. Other types of teacher-targeted humor utilize role-playing by the teacher that is related to the content (e.g., the teacher becomes Pythagoras while explaining the Pythagorean Theorem) or unrelated to course content (e.g., teacher mimics the voice of George Bush saying "read my lips" while giving directions). Finally, another example is when the teacher makes a self-deprecating remark (e.g., points out his/her own girth when teaching about proper diet).

Student-targeted humor is somewhat trickier to employ because of potential embarrassment and/or uneasiness on the part of the student. Examples of this type of humor include (a) joking good-naturedly about a student's erroneous response or comment, (b) insulting students in a friendly, nonhostile way (e.g., "this group enters the room like a herd of turtles"), (c) teasing students in a nonconfrontational way (e.g., referring to a junior high clique as the *Beverly Hills, 90210* group because of the clique's emulation of the cast of that show) and (d) student role-playing.

The third category is referred to as *untargeted humor* or, as Neulip points out, issue- or topic-oriented humor. This includes joke-telling, punning, tongue-in-cheek statements, and awkward comparisons/incongruity (e.g., using a *Far Side*–type drawing to illustrate amoebae interacting).

External sources of humor are the fourth category of the taxonomy. These include historical incidents with some humorous slant (e.g., the little girl who suggested that Abraham Lincoln grow a beard), third-party humor that is either related or unrelated to the content (e.g., cartoons, photographs, funny headlines, etc.), and natural phenomena (e.g., illustrating how creating a vacuum can cause a hard-boiled egg to be pushed into a narrow-necked milk bottle).

Finally, a teacher's use of nonverbal humor is the fifth category. This type of humor can be described as a *for effect* display (e.g., making a face to show feigned anger) or as part of physical humor to gain student attention through exaggerated gestures and other body movements.

Categories like these can be helpful in identifying the types of humor that teachers employ in the classroom. Although the categorization scheme was designed primarily for use with high school teachers, it can be applied to elementary classrooms.

Holt, Rinehart and Winston

The major difference in humor usage between the two settings may be one of degree rather than of kind. One would expect fewer and less-sophisticated examples of the types of humor described here, but one would still expect to find aspects of incongruity, joke-telling (riddles), physical humor, role-playing (pretend play), teasing, and so forth in the average elementary classroom.

During your observations in elementary, middle/junior high, and/or high school classrooms, you should become more adept at spotting humorous events, activities, statements, and so forth and at determining whether the use of humor was appropriate to the situation. The following Core Activity is designed to give you an instrument that you can use to identify the type, frequency, and appropriateness of humor in the classroom(s) that you're observing.

Core Activity

TEACHER HUMOR CHART

Use the following chart to categorize humorous incidents, activities, events, and so forth as you do your observations in an elementary or secondary classroom. Use one chart for each classroom that you observe (make copies of the chart if you observe more than one classroom) and indicate dates for each observation.

GRADE LEVEL: _____   DATES OF OBSERVATIONS: _____

SUBJECT(S) OBSERVED: _____

TEACHER GENDER: _____   ESTIMATED AGE OF TEACHER: _____

TEACHER-TARGETED HUMOR

CATEGORY	FREQUENCY	APPROPRIATE	INAPPROPRIATE
Self-disclosure related to content:			
Self-disclosure unrelated to content:			
Self-disclosure embarrassment:			
Teacher role-play related to content:			
Teacher role-play unrelated to content:			
Teacher self-deprecation:			

STUDENT-TARGETED HUMOR

CATEGORY	FREQUENCY	APPROPRIATE	INAPPROPRIATE
Error identification:			
Friendly insult:			
Teasing:			
Student role-play:			

UNTARGETED HUMOR

CATEGORY	FREQUENCY	APPROPRIATE	INAPPROPRIATE
Awkward comparison/ incongruity:			
Joke-telling:			
Punning:			
Tongue-in-cheek/ facetious:			

EXTERNAL SOURCE HUMOR

CATEGORY	FREQUENCY	APPROPRIATE	INAPPROPRIATE
Historical incidents:			
Third-party humor related to content (e.g., cartoons):			
Third-party humor unrelated to content:			
Natural phenomena humor:			

NONVERBAL HUMOR

CATEGORY	FREQUENCY	APPROPRIATE	INAPPROPRIATE
Affect display humor (e.g., exaggerated gestures or facial reactions):			
Kinesis humor:			

Questions for Discussion

1. Based on your observations, which types of humor were employed most frequently by elementary teachers? By secondary teachers? How do these totals compare with your expectations? Could the teacher(s) have employed humor more frequently? Less frequently? Explain.

2. To what extent was the use of humor appropriate to the situation, age of the students, subject/topic being taught, and personality of the teacher? What would you have done differently?

3. It has been suggested in some research studies that males use humor more frequently and more effectively than females and that students respond better to male teachers' humor. More recent studies, however, dispute this. What did you find in your observations when you compared them with your classmates'? Were there observable gender differences in terms of effective use of humor?

4. What differences in type of humor, frequency, and appropriateness did you find in classrooms of teachers who were under thirty years of age? Thirty-one to forty-five? Forty-six to sixty? Over sixty? Is age of the teacher an important factor to consider when studying humor in the classroom?

Throughout your experience as a learner in schools you probably encountered a number of teachers who used, or attempted to use, humor in their teaching. However, you may have had other memorably humorous experiences in school that occurred outside of the classroom. By and large, most critics of schools depict them as repressive, humorless places where little, if any, fun activities occur. Indeed, it often appears to such critics that teachers and school administrators consciously try to squelch humor in any form, whether teacher-targeted, student-targeted, student-generated, and so forth. In the following Suggested Activity, try to recall a person, incident, or event that you found to be memorably humorous. Try to identify the characteristics that made this person, incident, or event particularly humorous to you and, if possible, relate that to the categorization scheme mentioned previously.

Holt, Rinehart and Winston

Suggested Activity

FUNNY INCIDENTS IN SCHOOL

Describe in as much detail as possible:

1. The funniest person you knew in school:

2. The funniest teacher you knew in school:

3. The most humorous situation that you recall happening at school for which no one got into trouble:

4. The most humorous situation that you recall happening at school for which one or more persons got into trouble:

Holt, Rinehart and Winston

Student Name: _____   Date: _____

Journal Entry

During this observation you were asked to identify and categorize behaviors of teachers that were intended to be humorous. You were also asked to judge the appropriateness of the use of humor in the classroom. In this Journal Entry, try to analyze your own sense of humor and whether you could effectively use humor in your teaching. Suggest ways in which classrooms and schools might become places where humor is appreciated and utilized more frequently. Or, you may want to suggest ways in which humorous behavior (intentional and unintentional) can be reduced in classrooms.

_____

_____

_____

_____

_____

_____

_____

_____

_____

_____

_____

_____

_____

_____

_____

_____

_____

_____

_____

_____

References

Barnhart, N. C. (Winter 1989). Humor: An art in itself. *Delta Kappa Gamma Bulletin* 55, 9-12.

Bryant, J., Comisky, P., and Zillmann, D. (1979). Teachers' humor in the college classroom. *Communication Education* 28, 110-118.

Burt, L. M., and Sugawara, A. I. (1988). Children's humor and implications for teaching. *Early Childhood Development Care* 37, 13-25.

Gorham, J., and Christophel, D. M. (January 1990). The relationship of teachers' use of humor in the classroom to immediacy and student learning. *Communication Education* 39, 40-62.

Korobkin, D. (Fall 1988). Humor in the classroom: Considerations and strategies. *College Teaching* 36, 154-158.

McGhee, P. (1971). Development of the humor response: A review of literature. *Psychological Bulletin* 76, 328-348.

Nussbaum, J. F., Comadena, M. E., and Holladay, S. J. (May 1985). Verbal communication within the college classroom. Paper presented at the meeting of the International Communication Association, Chicago, Ill.

Neulip, J. W. (October 1991). An examination of the content of high school teachers' humor in the classroom and the development of an inductively derived taxonomy of classroom humor. *Communication Education* 40, 343-355.

Vance, C. M. (1987). Comparative study on humor and design of instruction. *Instructional Science* 16 (1): 79-100.

Ziv, A. (Fall 1988). Teaching and learning with humor, experiment and replication. *Journal of Experimental Education* 57, 5-15.

Holt, Rinehart and Winston

Chapter 9

THE TEACHER AND ETHICS

When we visit a school, or simply reflect upon our own experiences in school, we see people and buildings, books and charts, desks and chalkboards. All of these pieces are part of the intellectual mission of schools: to pass on to the next generation the knowledge they need to survive and to prosper. The observer can "see" this mission in action as teachers explain or drill and as students read or compute. The rituals and routines of school, from "paying attention" to taking tests, are oriented to this very apparent and obvious knowledge goal of schools.

Another mission of schools, although less obvious, is equally important. It goes by many names, such as "character education," "moral education," "education for citizenship," and "the teaching of values." Essentially, though, the mission is to ensure that young people acquire the ethical standards and enduring moral habits that they will need to manage their own lives and to contribute to the common good.

This moral mission of schools is not new. It is no late-twentieth-century fad. It goes to the very core of what it is to be educated, to be a person. Socrates said that the task of education is to make a person both smart and good. Many philosophers and thinkers have seen this ethical goal of education as even more fundamental than education's intellectual goal. Likewise, many parents are more concerned that their children are good than that they are smart. They want their children to grow up to be people with a clear sense of right and wrong, people who can be relied upon to do their share, to be loyal to their families and their nation, and to be honest in their dealings with others.

Fortunately, these two goals are not in conflict. It is not a matter of "either/or." Schools and teachers can and should help children develop knowledge (content and intellectual skills) as well as ethical values and positive character traits. The two goals should go hand in hand.

Some people who are considering careers in education may be uneasy with the idea of schools and teachers being involved in the moral education of the young. There is the question of exactly whose values should be taught, a question of particular concern to ethnic and religious minorities. In a highly pluralistic nation, such as the United States, it is important for the public school not to violate the ethical views of individual groups. Our tax-supported schools should not undermine the positive values taught in homes. But although teachers should be vigilant against that possibility, there are some strong arguments for teachers' active involvement in character formation and the acquisition of moral values. Consider the following:

169

Holt, Rinehart and Winston

- Great philosophers and thinkers from the ancients (Socrates, Plato, and Aristotle) to the moderns (John Dewey and John Goodlad) have taught that moral values and character development are a major part of education. Drawing on the Greek philosopher Aristotle, Jon Moline has written, "People do not naturally or spontaneously grow up to be morally excellent or practically wise. They become so, if at all, only as the result of a lifetime personal and community effort."

- Our nation's founding fathers (Jefferson, Franklin, and Madison) were anxious to create an education system that would teach and develop moral values, such as respect for the rights of others, personal responsibility, and tolerance, that are the foundation stones of a democratic society.

- The codes of education in the overwhelming majority of states explicitly point out that it is not simply the right of teachers, but indeed their responsibility to teach the values and moral habits that are so fundamental to good citizenship. In addition, the legislators in state after state in recent years, from New York to California, from New Hampshire to Oregon, have reaffirmed the need for schools to be more active and effective in this area.

- For almost twenty years, public opinion polls have demonstrated that four out of five Americans want public schools to take an active role in the moral education and character formation of the young. And the percentage is higher among those respondents who have children in public schools. In 1992 the Gallup organization asked, "Should the public schools teach the moral values that culturally divide us?"

Eighty-six percent of respondents reported that they were in favor of public schools teaching moral values, and only 12 percent were opposed.

It would appear, then, that there is a strong case and strong public support for the public schools taking an active and positive role in the moral education and character formation of students. Still, however, many educators are confused about how to proceed.

WHAT "PRODUCT" SHOULD THE PUBLIC SCHOOLS SEEK?

There is an old adage that you can't get to where you are going if you don't know where it is. This holds true, in general, for education and, in particular, for the moral and ethical goals of schooling. One way for teachers to conceive of this is to aim at developing a morally mature person. Working with a child's family, church, and community, educators see themselves contributing to the making of a person, to a "final product" who can think, feel, and act in a morally mature way. Said another way, the teacher should help her students know the good, love the good, and do the good.

Knowing the Good. Every community has a view of "the good life." Usually unstated, it is a vision of how people ought to live in order to be personally satisfied but also to be contributing members of that society. It is a fundamental task of the schools to help children perceive that vision of the good life and learn how to attain it. Anthropologists and social psychologists, who study how people live together in groups, might describe this effort as the adults of a community socializing the young into the morality of the tribe. Without this shared vision of what is right and what is wrong, the society begins to fall apart. This shared vision can also be described as a moral literacy. Morally literate people know, for instance, that they ought to:

- Be honest in their dealings with others
- Respect the rights of others
- Behave responsibly in their work and to those around them
- Be concerned with the underdogs and those less fortunate than they

Morally literate people should know these *should*s and how they contribute to a better life.

True teachers are not interested in developing children into simple "rule-keepers." Therefore, it is important that students know how to think through moral and ethical issues. They must be able to think through questions such as: "What is the right thing to do in this situation?" "What are the consequences of this course of action or that course of action?" As citizens, graduates of our schools must be able to fulfill the requirements of democratic citizenship. They must be able to select the most ethical solutions to civic problems, solutions that both protect the individual and serve the common good. Teachers, then, need to be in continual dialogue with students if they are to know the good.

Loving the Good.   Life is not all "sweet reason." When we make moral decisions and ethical choices, our emotions and desires have a strong influence on us. The heart, then, is a crucial element in moral education. If a child is totally in love with himself—that is, if he is truly "selfish"—he is a danger to himself and those around him. One of the important functions of the school, therefore, is to help children love the right things—the right people, the right ideas, and the right actions.

As teachers, then, we must touch the heart. Warren Nord has stated it nicely: "The relationship between feeling and reason in ethics is complex and controversial, but certainly morality is grounded to some considerable extent in the moral feelings—compassion, guilt, hope, despair, dignity, mercy, and love, for example. When ethics is stripped of its emotional dimensions, it becomes artificial, abstract, and lifeless." It is the work of education, then, to help the child love the right things and especially the right image of himself or herself.

Doing the Good.   To know the good and to love the good are important, but behavior is the bottom line. What we actually do is the true criterion of moral persons. Many of us can intellectually come up with the morally right course of action and even want to do the right thing, but doing what is right is the acid test. For instance, on the school bus, when other children are making life miserable for another child, a particular student may know what the right thing to do is and may even want to stop the teasing and meanness, but he may simply let them happen.

Implicit in this expectation that the school help children do the good is the need for teachers to help children practice moral action. Teachers, then, must set up opportunities for students to do the good. They must help the young engage in moral action and help them acquire the enduring habits that make good character. They must give them opportunities to practice the "good life" that they come to know through stories and instruction. They must help students not simply to know how important it is for citizens to be responsible, but also to behave responsibly.

Helping the student become a morally mature person is a slow process. It is, also, quite different from first grade to middle school to high school. To ignore this domain, however, is impossible. The school cannot host children from the time that they are five until seventeen and eighteen and not profoundly affect how they think and feel about issues of right and wrong. School, with all its rewards and punishments and social tugging and towing, cannot help but have a strong moral impact on students. Like it or not, moral education—for good or ill—is an inevitable part of school.

WHAT CAN SCHOOLS AND TEACHERS DO?

The school is a swirling cauldron of moral matter: students bullying one another, teachers gossiping, students volunteering to help a classmate, teachers staying after school to work with a child returning after an illness, teachers playing favorites, students writing graffiti in the lavatories, and on and on. Inevitably, the school sends powerful moral messages to the student. The matter, however, should not be left to chance. The classroom and the school can positively affect the moral maturity of the student in specific ways. What follows, then, are the authors' "five *E*s of moral and character education"—*example*, *explanation*, *exhortation*, *ethos*, and *experience*.

Example.   Although the expectation that, as teachers, we must be "good examples" to our students may be unsettling to many of us (even paralyzing us with fear), there is really no way around this fact. Students spend long hours during the all-important formative period of their lives in close-up observation of teachers. The unseen, but ever-present "project" of a child is to become a successful adult.

Anyone who has ever had children in school or who has listened to students talk about their teachers knows that students only occasionally concern themselves with their teachers' instructional strategies or skills. Whether or not the teacher uses audiovisual materials well or can use a variety of questioning techniques is rarely commented on. Students do, however, complain about and praise the teacher's moral qualities. "She is so unfair!" "Last year my teacher played favorites, but Miss Kinsella treats everyone the same." "At the beginning of the year Mr. Oliver said that he would stay after school and help anyone having difficulties, and he really means it."

A few years ago, there was a cartoon in *New Yorker* magazine that depicted a fifth-grade student telling her stunned father, "What did we learn in school today? We learned that Paris is cool. Amsterdam is groovy. And that Miss Fisher isn't going to marry that guy in the black leather jacket who picks her up every day after school with his motorcycle." Although Miss Fisher's lesson plan may have said that the day's educational goals were to teach long division and how deserts are formed, the enduring lessons may have been quite different.

The great English parliamentarian and social philosopher Edmund Burke once wrote, "Example is the school of mankind, and they will learn at no other." Teachers are de facto moral exemplars or models in numerous ways, from our thoughtfulness toward those around us to the way we react to students' cheating. Perhaps the most powerful way that we teach moral values is the way that is least discussed: the way that we do our work.

Whether surgeons or shoemakers or second-grade teachers, people have a moral responsibility to be excellent at their craft. Although the surgeon's work is hidden, and the shoemaker's seams unseen, the teacher's craft is continually on display. We instill moral education by:

- the way we prepare our lessons and classes
- the promptness and thoroughness with which we correct papers and exams
- the care we take to see that students are actually learning
- our lack of tolerance for wasting time
- the accuracy of our grades and records
- the effort we give to those who need more advanced work and those who need special help
- being a learner and keeping up with our field
- the standards we set for ourselves and our students

Another way that teachers teach good values and important character traits is through the curriculum. One way to view the school's curriculum is as society's choice of what is most worth knowing. Prominent among this mass of ideas, skills, and information are the individual people who have contributed to our progress and success and those who have betrayed their responsibilities to those around them. So history and biography are important components of schooling. Our children must know from our own national heritage: Thomas Jefferson, Benedict Arnold, Abraham Lincoln, Harriet Tubman, Andrew Carnegie, Jane Addams, Huey Long, Franklin and Eleanor Roosevelt. They must know, too, the moral examples in our literature because these characters are frequently the embodiment of our ethical ideals. They learn courage from *The Scarlet Letter's* Hester Prynne; the price of hypocrisy from the book's Arthur Dimmesdale. When Huck Finn's struggles with his conscience over whether or not to turn in the runaway slave, Jim, students learn that the established laws and public views are not always correct. From *To Kill a Mockingbird's* Atticus Finch, they learn how a morally mature individual meets his responsibilities to his family, his neighbors, and his community. Although this moral dimension of literature is often ignored, it is a powerful conveyor of our society's moral ideals and exemplars.

Explanation.   Knowing the good means that we understand what is right and correct. A child needs to learn that punching someone who frustrates him is not a good way to behave. He needs to learn why he cannot spread lies about another student or cheat on an examination. Through fear and punishment, students can be trained to behave, but after they are out of school, their behavior may revert to settling matters by these antisocial methods unless they understand why standards exist.

Knowing the good means that we can think through issues of right and wrong and come up with ethical decisions. This intellectual skill does not just happen. Much of what a teacher does is explaining. She explains cause and effect. She explains the need to get the facts. She explains how to draw correct conclusions. She explains our society's rules and why and how we look out for the underdog. And she explains why and how we follow our Constitution. Critical thinking and reasoning skills have a great deal to do with citizenship and our moral lives. The work of the teacher, then, involves explaining not only the content of our social rules, but also the process. Students need to be able to think through the ethical issues that they will inevitably face as adults and as citizens.

Exhortation.   The *exhortation* that we write of is an exhortation to the heart. As suggested earlier, there are times when sweet reason fails. The children on the bus continue to pick on one, lonely child. They understand why it is not a good thing to make the child so unhappy. Each knows that he or she should buck the crowd and "do the right thing." But they do not. There are students who confront terrible problems like physical handicaps to divorcing parents. They are depressed and discouraged. Like the children on the bus, they can see no reason to change their attitude. It is here that the teacher needs to make an appeal to the heart, to that image that each child has of the good person each wants to be. Whether it is a pep talk or a stern reminder, it appeals emotionally to this moral ideal. And although this exhortation should never be far from rational explanation, it is essentially an appeal to the heart.

An important foundation for these appeals to the heart is helping children develop an image of the good person, the ideal self that can be appealed to. This is another reason for children to have storehouses of "good examples" or personal heroes in their minds. To the degree that our heroes and heroines are understood and admired, they exert a positive pull on us.

Another aspect of this appeal to the heart is the ability to empathize. Morally mature individuals are able "to walk in the shoes of the people they meet." They feel the suffering of others and the injustice that others are experiencing. They can put themselves into the place of the child who is being mistreated by her bus mates. They can understand what it feels like to be a slave. There is something inside these students to which the teacher can direct his exhortations.

Ethos.   *Ethos* is a word of Greek origin that refers to the character or the distinguishing attitudes and habits of a place or a person. Like a prison or a training camp, a school has an ethos. This ethos is unseen, but it is also a powerful influence on those present. The ethos of a place says what kind of behavior is encouraged or tolerated in that place. It speaks to the standards of the place, the qualities of the human relations among people, and what is rewarded and what is punished. (Another "*E*" word is *environment*, as in "the moral environment of the place.")

Most experienced educators can enter a school building, whether elementary or secondary, urban or suburban, public or private, and rather quickly get a sense of the moral ethos. There is a moral climate that is sensed in the way that people address one another. Sullen students, aloof teachers, and hostile staff reflect one kind of ethos. Engaged students, involved teachers, and courteous staff are strong indicators of attitudes and personal habits that are part of a positive moral ethos. In recent years, much has been written about the "hidden curriculum" of the school—that is, all of the learnings that are not written down in the formal documents of the school but still get taught there—such as learning not to tell the teacher what you *really* thought of the first act of *King Lear* or how to avoid gym on those days when you are really feeling awful. These true learnings are part of the hidden curriculum. But so, too, are the attitudes and moral standards that we absorb from the moral climate of the school.

Although a school's "ethos" sounds like a vague abstraction that would be out of the control of an educator, just the opposite is true. There are classroom teachers who have made their rooms a safe haven and a productive work scene in schools that are otherwise chaotic. And there are classrooms where students have become

Holt, Rinehart and Winston

hostile and aggressive in schools that are otherwise cooperative and relaxed. The point is that the classroom ethos or school ethos is made. It is a place where there are fair rules, evenly enforced. It is a place where there is an air of responsibility that is shared by all. Typically, ethos is the product of the professional staff working together to create a certain kind of climate. But whether or not a school has a morally positive ethos, we can be sure of one thing: Ethos teaches.

Experience.   We live in a world of images and symbols. For many children, television is their primary window onto reality. We also live in a world where there are limited out-of-school opportunities to work. Modern life seems to have conspired to keep many children from real encounters with life, ones that make serious demands on them and from which they can grow into confident adults. In an earlier era, the young man learning farming at his father's side, or the older sister living in a large family had demands thrust upon them. And although many of the changes in modern life have been quite positive, modern life has robbed the young of many of the maturing experiences of the past. James Coleman, a distinguished sociologist, has stated that "American youth are information rich and experience poor." It is impossible to become a fully developed adult without maturing experiences.

A primary task of schools is to work with family and community to help children become contributing members of society. "Contributing members" means people who look out for others, who think of themselves as helpers, and who have the skills needed to be of help to others. School is an ideal place for children both to learn that they ought to be helpers and to learn how to be helpers. Although learning that they "ought" to contribute to others and the common good is discussed earlier, learning is our subject here.

Children learn how to be helpers by structured activities, such as:

- A carefully monitored cooperative activity, where they are shown how to be of direct aid to one another
- Having a specific task to perform regularly, which benefits the class or the school (that is, feeding the gerbil and cleaning its cage or picking up trash in a certain area)
- Volunteering to help the teacher or librarian as an aide, doing clerical or routine tasks for them
- Being part of a class that once a month helps out an elderly couple having trouble keeping up with their house
- Taking on a community service project, such as spending an afternoon each week reading to the blind

Students can learn the skills of being a contributor through unstructured experiences, such as:

- Helping another student who is having difficulty with an assignment
- Befriending a new or lonely student
- Being a peacemaker between warring friends or groups
- Standing up against injustice, such as playground bullying or students
- Unfairly spreading rumors about another student

Although knowing the good and loving the good are important, doing the good is, in effect, where the rubber meets the road. Moral actions are not only what we should be aiming for in school, but they are also the means. The philosopher

Aristotle claimed that a person becomes virtuous (that is, a person of good habits) by doing good things. We become brave by doing brave acts. We become kind by doing kind acts. Teachers, then, must make sure that there are opportunities, structured and unstructured, for students to become "moral actors."

Although values and "character" cannot be seen, the classroom or school that is attending to its moral mission has certain observable qualities. These qualities are our five *E*s of moral and character education.

The teacher, by definition, is involved with a deeply ethical enterprise. Henry Adams wrote, "A teacher affects eternity: no one can tell where his influence stops." The work of the teacher involves subject matter and instructional technique, but all of this is permeated by the ethical. We find ourselves asking:

- "What are the important moral ideas in this story or in this historical event?"
- "What are the reasons why I insist that children respect one another and not fight or use crude language?"
- "Why don't I allow cheating, and why do I insist on honesty?"
- "Why am I so concerned that my top students are so terribly competitive?"
- "What am I going to do to make George less selfish?"

In all of these questions, we are recognizing the intricate moral nature of classrooms. But unlike the intellectual nature and the knowledge mission, it is woven into the very fabric of schooling. And for this reason it is important for the future teacher to look at schools and classrooms through the lens of the school's ethical and character-forming missions.

Holt, Rinehart and Winston

Have a private conversation with the teacher whom you have been observing, or a teacher of your acquaintance, about his or her perception of the role of a moral educator. Generate a list of your own questions but consider using some of these:

1. Do you consciously try to teach and promote certain moral values in your class-room? Which ones? How do you do it?

2. Are there moral values that you would like to teach but that you think are inap-propriate for public schools? Why?

3. What good habits are you trying to promote in your classroom?

4. Have you ever received support or encouragement from parents for stressing moral values and issues of character? Have you ever encountered problems or objections?

5. What is a serious ethical issue with which you have been confronted in the class-room? In this school?

6. Do other teachers in this school discuss the ethical and moral aspects of their work with children? Do you feel encouragement or support from your adminis-trators?

Provide your own questions about moral and character education in the space provided.

Core Activity

STUDENT OBSERVATION ACTIVITY

Over a period of thirty minutes, focus exclusively on the moral dimension of a student's experience. In the space that follows, jot down observational notes about the influences on and activities affecting the student. Try to keep your notes descriptive and not judgmental. To help you sort out the experience, we suggest that you organize your notes under the headings of the five *E*s described earlier.

1. Examples:
   Teacher
   Other students
   People in the curriculum (in stories or in discussions of current events)

   Other examples (pictures of famous people on the walls)

2. Explanations:
   Teacher talk about rules or discipline or ethical issues

Holt, Rinehart and Winston

Student talk about rules or other ethical issues

Direct teaching about what is the correct thing to do

3. Exhortations:
   Direct appeals by teachers to do the right thing (or to "desist from doing the wrong thing")

Praise or scolding for certain behaviors

Holt, Rinehart and Winston

4. Ethos:
   What in the moral climate of this classroom helps or hinders the moral learning of
   the student?

   What are the signs of a "healthy" or "unhealthy" moral environment?

5. Experiences:
   Is there evidence of moral action in this classroom? _____

   Are there opportunities to be helpful? _____ Are students encouraged to
   be helpful? _____ Do they take the opportunities? _____

   Does this class have opportunities for students to practice selfish or mean-spirited
   activities against one another? _____

6. Other:

Suggested Activity 2

THE MORAL ENVIRONMENT CHECKLIST

Based on your observation of the school in which you are observing, fill in the following checklist of activities and programs that have been associated with a school having a strong moral environment.

1. There is a recognition program for positive conduct (i.e., service to others).

   _____

2. Students and their parents get regular feedback on the moral dimension of their school experience (e.g., marks for conduct).

   _____

3. The halls and classrooms display pictures of cultural heroes and/or inspirational sayings.

   _____

4. The school has a mission statement that includes the moral domain.

   _____

5. There is a written code of conduct for this classroom/school, and the students are well aware of it.

   _____

6. There are effective student organizations that directly promote responsible conduct (e.g., SADD).

   _____

7. There is regular evidence of mutual respect observable in this school.

   _____

Student Name: _____ Date: _____

Journal Entry

In this Journal Entry, focus upon schools and classrooms as environments for character and moral education. Pay particular attention to the role that the teacher plays as well as to how moral and ethical issues are integrated into the curriculum.

_____

_____

_____

_____

_____

_____

_____

_____

_____

_____

_____

_____

_____

_____

_____

_____

_____

_____

_____

_____

_____

_____

_____

_____

_____

Holt, Rinehart and Winston

_____

_____

_____

_____

_____

_____

_____

_____

_____

_____

_____

_____

_____

_____

_____

_____

_____

_____

_____

_____

_____

_____

_____

_____

_____

Questions for Discussion

1. What should be the role of the school in helping students identify, clarify, or modify their values?

2. How do the moral and character-formation needs of children vary from elementary to middle to high school?

3. Are there some content areas better suited for presenting moral/ethical dilemmas to students? If so, which ones, and why do you believe they are better suited for this role?

4. What role does the teacher play in providing a model for students in terms of moral and ethical behavior? Should teachers be hired and/or tenured on the basis of their ability to provide an appropriate model for students?

5. Based on your observations, which, if any, of the "five *E*s" of moral and character education currently exist in schools? Which appear to be more powerful? Which need to be incorporated more fully into schools?

6. Are there ethical/moral issues too controversial for teachers to discuss with students? If so, which ones? How did the teachers you observed handle controversial issues? Did you agree with them?

Holt, Rinehart and Winston

Chapter 10

EMBRACING THE CHALLENGE OF DIVERSITY AND INDIVIDUAL DIFFERENCES IN AMERICAN CLASSROOMS

Currently, when individuals choose to become teachers they make a positive statement about themselves vis-à-vis diversity. Today, classroom teachers routinely face increased diversity in terms of students' ethnicity, linguistic and cultural backgrounds, family structures, socioeconomic status, intellectual aptitude, technological resources, learning styles, and degree of learning handicap. And, as the Davidmans note, "more diversity and complexity appear to be inevitable as increased numbers of immigrants from around the world seek out their part in the American drama, and teachers work with families suffering from new levels of economic deprivation" (1997). As an example of the latter, we have the Vaughn Street Elementary School in San Fernando, California, where the principal, Yvonne Chan, used a foundation grant to install washing machines and showers at her school so that homeless students could take care of basic necessities. At the same school other grants were utilized to establish a family center where families without health insurance could bring their children to have their eyes and ears checked and where parents could participate in programs aimed at improving their self-esteem (Jones, 1992).

The teaching profession has not ignored this reality. In all fifty states, in more than twelve hundred teacher training programs, and in approximately sixteen thousand school districts educators have accepted, with varying degrees of commitment, the responsibility of educating highly diverse groups and individuals to their fullest potential. This commitment to support equity and diversity is part of the tradition, legislative framework, and sometimes merely the symbolic rhetoric of American education (Kozol, 1991) and advanced capitalistic democracy. The latter notwithstanding, this tradition is what makes the American classroom unique among the classrooms of the world—at least in the potential that it holds for the physically challenged, the culturally different, and the poverty afflicted. For future teachers it is particularly noteworthy that data provided by the National Center for Children in Poverty (NCCP) in 1992 revealed that (a) the poor included 26 percent of all American children under the age of six (more than one in four) and 20 percent of all children between the ages of six and seventeen and (b) in both cases the twenty-year trend line (1972–1992) reveals increasing numbers of children living in poverty. For

185

Holt, Rinehart and Winston

example, in 1972 17 percent of all American children under six, and 15 percent of those between six and seventeen, lived in poverty (*News and Issues,* 1995). In addition the 1992 NCCP database showed that although African American and Hispanic children under six comprised 29 percent of the total number of American children under six, they were 55 percent of the total number of poor children in this category. Thus, in 1992 African American and Hispanic children under six were nearly twice as likely to be poor as were white children under six, and this ratio was consistent with data collected by the U.S. Bureau of the Census in 1990 (Chiarelott et al., 1994). The moral of this statistical story is that learning how to reach, teach, and inspire impoverished learners will be a major chunk of the *diversity* challenge facing future teachers in twentieth- and twenty-first-century classrooms.

Such classrooms, filled with new levels of complexity and diversity, have the potential to make teaching a fascinating and emotionally rewarding career. But, diversity can cut two ways. It can be challenging and rewarding, but it can also be frightening and overwhelming. Although your teacher education program will gradually provide you with skills and knowledge to meet the challenge of diversity, your own personality, attitudes, and willingness to develop new skills will play a major role in defining the way in which diversity affects your career. Are you willing, *por ejemplo*, to become a second *lengua* learner yourself at this early stage in your professional development?

With the importance of modeling in mind, some of the activities in this chapter will introduce you to teachers who provide positive examples of successfully embracing the challenge of diversity, whereas other activities will heighten your awareness of specific elements of diversity. However, before delineating the activities, we will briefly discuss some of the key terms associated with diversity in the literature and classrooms that you will encounter. Our remarks will prepare you for the variety of definitions that exist as well as for the activities that follow and any interviews that you choose to develop related to content in this chapter. The terms that we will address are: *multicultural education, multiethnic education, educational equity, special education, mainstreaming, education for the gifted and talented, bilingual/bicultural education, at-risk learners, learning styles,* and *social construction of knowledge.* This is an imposing list of terms, and several of the terms have more than one meaning. With this in mind, Figure 10.1 includes a strategy that we call *multiperspective teaching of American, Canadian, Mexican, and world history,* and please note that we could have substituted many other specific nations, such as Japan, Nigeria, and Russia, because multiperspective teaching applies to all nations, indeed, all content. Multiperspective teaching is based on two ideas and is related to a third, namely the social construction of knowledge. First, there is the idea that individuals and groups will often have different views about a particular event or explanation because of the culture and era of which they are a part. Second, there is the idea that it is liberating and wise for students to learn history in a manner that consistently exposes them to these various, and often competing, perspectives.

As students study history in this manner they develop an implicit awareness of a key multicultural education concept—the aforementioned social construction of knowledge. What is left implicit for students needs to be made explicit here for future teachers. As the Davidmans note:

> The idea that knowledge is a social construction, and more specifically that social and
> bureaucratic concepts and categories like race, ethnicity, exceptionality, socioeconomic
> status, gender, and religion are based on subjective criteria invented by human beings, is

critically important for teachers and students to comprehend as they develop their moral vision and voice (1997).

And it is not only these terms and categories that are social inventions; other terms that we will define later, like *multicultural education*, *multiethnic education*, *bilingual education*, *educational equity*, and *mainstreaming*, also are socially constructed. As Mary Kay Thompson Tetreault reminds us, all of these terms, indeed, "all works in literature, science, and history . . . have an author—male or female, white or ethnic or racial minority, elite or middle-class or occasionally poor—with motivations and beliefs" (1993, p. 130).

We share these observations because we believe that awareness of them will quite properly leave future teachers more inclined to question the concepts, assumptions, and knowledge claims of various authority figures such as media pundits, political and religious leaders, college professors, and textbook writers. Such questioning is an essential component of the curriculum reform movement known as multicultural education, as well as of the knowledge base and temperament underlying what American colleges call the "liberal arts."

Thus, at the same time that we define some basic multicultural terms, we remind you that there are other definitions of these terms—and indeed other critical terms—that we do not share, no doubt for reasons that we see and don't see, reasons that are linked to our sociocultural identities. Now, with social construction confessions made, and with humility, let us turn to our definitions.

Within the set, multicultural education has the broadest sweep, and several writers see it as an educational movement that subsumes all the terms listed earlier. It is also an emergent concept and since the 1960s has been defined in several interesting ways. Several definitions emphasize cultural pluralism (Grant, 1977), while

"Of course it's misspelled. I'm preserving my indigenous cultural dialect."

Holt, Rinehart and Winston

others emphasize educational equity (Banks, 1981). More recently, antiracist education and critical pedagogy (Nieto, 1992) and freedom (Banks, 1993) have been included as critical components. In an attempt to create a practical synthesis conception, Patricia and Leonard Davidman have defined *multicultural education* as

> ... a multifaceted change-oriented strategy that is aimed at seven interrelated goals. These goals are:
>
> 1. Educational equity
> 2. Empowerment of students and their parents
> 3. Cultural pluralism in society
> 4. Intergroup and intragroup understanding and harmony in the classroom and school community
> 5. An expanded knowledge base of cultural and ethnic groups
> 6. The development of students and practitioners (teachers, nurses, administrators, counselors, etc.) whose thoughts and actions are guided by an informed multicultural perspective
> 7. Freedom/the maintenance and extension of democracy (1977).

These goals can be achieved by a wide range of strategies which can be seen in Figures 10.1 and 10.2. Below is a visual summary of the preceding synthesis conception.

Despite the inevitable conceptual conflict in the multicultural education literature, which is one outcome of the social construction of knowledge process, almost all writers on this topic agree that multicultural education has been a catalyst for reform in American education and that the 1954 Supreme Court decision in *Brown*

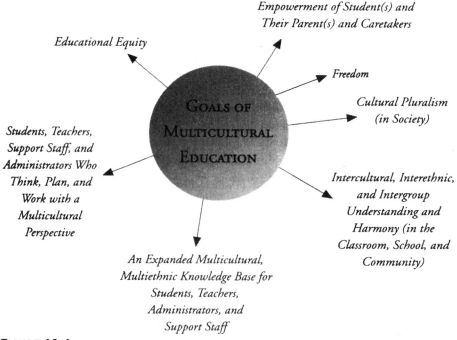

FIGURE 10–1

Holt, Rinehart and Winston

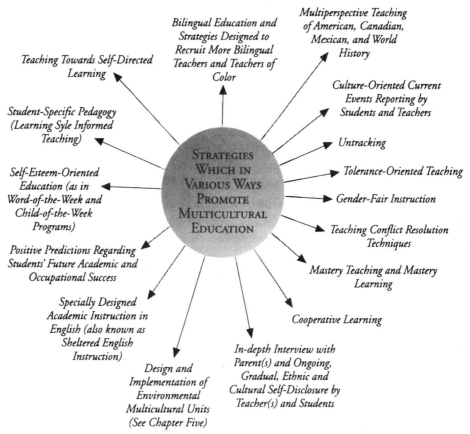

FIGURE 10-2

v. the Board of Education (of Topeka, Kansas) was a decisive point in this reform movement. The major goal of this movement has been to create educational equity for a wide range of cultural and ethnic groups, and these cultural groups have included women, the learning disabled and physically challenged (handicapped), and, more recently, gay and lesbian learners. Ethnic groups—cultural groups with a common history and sense of peoplehood—who have been oppressed in American history have always been a major focus of advocates of multiculturalism. These groups, which have been differentially impacted by prejudice and racism in American culture, include African Americans, American Indians, and some but not all Hispanic Americans and Asian Americans. James Banks (1981) and others (Gay, 1983) have gone to great lengths to make certain that these groups do not get lost amidst the variety of groups falling under the umbrella of multicultural education. Toward this end Banks created the concept of *multiethnic education* to complement multicultural education. Multiethnic education complements multicultural education by keeping uppermost in educators' minds the importance of combating fascism in American society and all of its manifestations in American schools.

Educational equity, in the earlier discussion, implies the opportunity to study in schools that are equally funded and dedicated to creating optimal academic success for all students. More specifically the Davidmans have defined *educational equity* in terms of three observable conditions: (a) physical and financial conditions, (b) the opportunity to learn, and (c) educational outcomes for both individuals and groups (1997, p. 14). Thus, when educators strive to create equity in a classroom or school, they try to make the following roughly equivalent (exact numerical equality is a social and bureaucratic impossibility):

1. Physical conditions in which children learn
2. Quality and experience of teachers and administrators
3. Opportunity that various types of learners have to learn
4. And most controversially, the educational achievement of various groups within the class, school, and school district (e.g., boys and girls, black, white, and Hispanic Americans, monolingual and bilingual learners, the economically impoverished, and those more fortunate)

Despite the clarity in the preceding definition, creating educational equity in public schools remains elusive, and the concept, for a variety of reasons, remains ambiguous for teachers and administrators. The social construction of knowledge process, because it tends to produce competing conceptions of reality, contributes to the ambiguity, although this need not be the case. When educators understand the knowledge construction process they will better understand, first, the inevitability of conceptual conflict, and second, their responsibility to work their way out of confusion with their own critical thinking, definitions, and synthesis conceptions of reality. Let us briefly examine some competing conceptions of educational equity to see how such synthesizing might work.

To begin with, we have the theorizing of Kenneth Sirotnick. For Sirotnick, "equity is concerned with the allocation of resources to *groups*, is assessed quantitatively, and is conceptually linked to the idea of excellence" (Davidman and Davidman, 1997, p. 78). And excellence, Sirotnick notes, is indicated by "conditions, practices, and outcomes in school that are associated with high levels of learning for most students in all valued goal areas of the common curriculum" (1990, p. 159). Based on this perspective, Sirotnick writes: "Equity is indicated when there are no systematic differences in the distributions of these conditions, practices, and outcomes based upon race, ethnicity, economic status, or any other irrelevant grouping characteristic" (1990, p. 159). The big idea here for our purposes is that when Sirotnick thinks about educational equity, he thinks about *cultural* and *ethnic groups* and ways to bring the academic achievement of these groups closer together. This, parenthetically, is the dominant perspective on educational equity.

In contrast to the group-oriented theorizing of Sirotnick, we have the equity theorizing of Elliot Eisner. Eisner, who constructs his conception of equity from deep within an individualistic perspective, states first not only that "equity is achieved in education by giving students an opportunity to come to school, but also that it is influenced by what they find when they arrive. School programs that create a very narrow eye of the needle through which all children must pass diminish educational equity," and second that "The genuinely good school does not diminish individual differences, it expands them" (1991, p. 17). So, we have here two conceptions of educational equity, conceptions that point us in different directions. One is concerned with diminishing academic achievement differences between racial, gender, and socioeconomic groups; the other is concerned with individual learners and the creation of school curricula that allow these learners to become their own idiosyncratic unique selves and as different as they can possibly become. Although these conceptions can be treated as antithetical to each other, it is also possible for each to contain truths that educators can embrace to create schools that are fair for individuals on the one hand and for groups that have been oppressed and stigmatized by social forces such as racism, sexism, and homophobia on the other. Indeed, teachers in American society, who will deal with *real* individuals in all of their diversity and real social groups in all of their complexity, need "... more than an either-or conception of equity. They need a conception that helps them to work wisely and fairly with both individuals and groups and a philosophy that enables them to do this without trampling on the constitutional rights of individuals or groups" (Davidman and Davidman, 1977, pp. 79–80).

The conception of educational equity that teachers in our society need will flexibly draw upon Eisner and Sirotnick, will include quantitative and qualitative elements such as those discussed by Geneva Gay (1993, p. 189), but will also need new ideas and practices to advance the equity agenda. We all need a conception of equity that begins not with schools and *educational* equity, but rather with society and social equity (or social justice), one that ultimately integrates educational equity and social justice in a manner that is meaningful for classroom teachers. This integrated conception will remind teachers that it is society that creates fair schools and not the other way around, and that it is futile to focus exclusively on school-based equity issues in a society in which inequality is a deep structural value. In other words, guided by the integrated conception, teachers will be challenged to simultaneously work on equity/fairness issues in society and school. And when they do this, they will come head to head with strategies and controversies related to *bilingual education* and *special education*.

On a national scale, bilingual education and *special education* are key components of the equity, or fairness, movement; furthermore, at the classroom level of operation both can be construed as legislated teaching strategies that help to achieve specific goals of multicultural education, most notably educational equity and empowerment of students and parents. Although the relationship between multicultural education, special education, and bilingual education is clear to many, you will also encounter situations where the autonomy of special education and bilingual education is emphasized. This occurs primarily because each was created by federal legislation. In 1973 in *Lau v. Nichols*, a class action suit filed on behalf of Chinese-speaking students in San Francisco schools, the U.S. Supreme Court ruled that schools must provide special language programs for students who don't understand or speak English and that these special programs do not include total sink-or-swim submission as the only alternative available. Relatedly, in a 1975 decision that affected every school and school district in the nation, Congress passed Public Law (PL) 94-142, Education for all Handicapped Children. This law stipulated that handicapped children must be educated in the environment that is least restrictive to their learning. In the two decades following this pioneering legislation, Congress has added amendments to the original legislation, and in 1990 in PL 101-476 changed the name of the law to the Individuals with Disabilities Education Act.

As a result of PL 94-142, in public school settings special educators have additional training and special licenses and are responsible for establishing fair and optimal learning environments for students who have learning disabilities or more serious physical challenges such as deafness, blindness, and various forms of brain damage. Mainstreaming, a broad strategy that attempts to provide the least-restrictive (or most optimal) learning environment by bringing special education students into regular education classrooms (the mainstream), is a movement that continues to expand. For example, in 1987 the Severely Handicapped Branch of the Federal Office of Special Education funded five states (California, Colorado, Kentucky, Virginia, and Illinois) to undertake pilot projects that would significantly increase the number of students with severe disabilities who were being educated in an "integrated" learning environment—a new term for the contemporary mainstream classroom environment. By 1991 sixteen states had pilot projects under way (P. Karasoff, personal communication, October 1991), and in the 1990s these projects became part of a national movement known as *inclusion*. The major difference between traditional mainstreaming and inclusion is that in the former the presumption is that the least-restrictive environment for the wide range of special learners with physical challenges and/or learning disabilities *may* be the integrated mainstream classroom or the segregated special day classroom or some combination of both. Inclusion supporters, in contrast, believe that the mainstream class *is* the least-restrictive environment for the vast majority of these special learners and that it should be every family's right to choose this classroom for their children.

When children who fall under the protection of PL 94-142 and PL 101-476 are placed into a mainstreamed or more restricted environment or some combination thereof, an individual educational plan (IEP) will be drawn up by a team of educators and the school site administrator in consultation with the children's parent(s) or caretaker(s). Increasingly, these mandatory IEPs attempt to take into account the students' learning style and preferences as the school site team identifies specific goals and learning activities for the children in question. As used here *learning style* means, and consists of, those variables that describe the way that an individual prefers to learn difficult information. When these variables are folded into a child's learning environment, his or her academic aptitude and performance will increase. Examples of learning style variables include the time of day when a child will take a course, the type of lighting in a room, the presence and degree of cooperative learning in a classroom, the opportunity to listen to chapters in a text as opposed to an exclusive reliance on a print material, and the presence of a very structured, demanding teacher as opposed to a low-pressure learning environment characterized by lots of opportunity for self-directed learning. It is noteworthy that many students will benefit from one or more of these variables but can be successful learners without them. For these learners the variables are instructional preferences. In contrast, for other learners the presence or absence of a variable will have a more dramatic effect. It is when these variables are almost a biological or cultural need that they are properly perceived as part of an individual's deep learning style.

Bilingual education in the contemporary curriculum, as noted, was given legal support by the U.S. Supreme Court in 1973, but it has been a part of American public education since the nineteenth century when German-speaking students received daily instruction in English and German. Today, the term *bilingual education* means many things, but at a general level it is best understood ". . . as an educational program that involves the use of two languages of instruction at some point in a student's school career" (Nieto, 1992). The recipient will typically, but not always, be a second language learner who (in America) is learning English as a second language. In the upside-down world of education, when English speakers (in America) learn a second language it is typically referred to as foreign language instruction, unless, of course, it is the student's native tongue.

Some of the major types of bilingual education are transitional bilingual education, maintenance bilingual education, and bilingual/bicultural education. In the maintenance approach the goal is to produce students who will be functionally

Holt, Rinehart and Winston

bilingual, whereas in the transitional approach students move into an English-only program as soon as possible with no consideration given to bilinguality. In either of the preceding, when the learners' native culture as well as language are made part of the curriculum, we have an approach that is sometimes called *bilingual/bicultural education* (Nieto, 1992).

For the reader, the critical point is that bilingual education—and related terms like *limited English proficient* (LEP), *English as a second language* (ESL), *specially designed academic instruction in English* (SDAIE), and *sheltered English instruction*—points to a significant dimension of diversity in our nation. The current wave of immigration into the United States is bringing hundreds of thousands of second language learners into the classes that you will teach. These new Americans are coming into schools that no longer try to melt away all of their cultural differences; indeed, utilization of these differences, along with a strong emphasis on English literacy and a weaker emphasis on bilingualism, is part and parcel of the complex equation of multicultural education. This is an equation to which you will inevitably contribute, and the sooner you sort out your attitudes, the better. Parenthetically, with attitudes in mind, it is instructive that certain states, like California, now use the term *English learner* rather than *limited English proficient*. They believe that the former has less negative connotation.

Another controversial term associated with individual differences in aptitude and academic performance is *gifted and talented*. Often perceived as part of the special education continuum, gifted and talented programs try to create optimal learning environments for students whose intellectual aptitude and rate of learning are extraordinarily high. Some educators believe that these students are penalized when they are kept exclusively in the regular education program with students and teachers who possess a different intellectual capacity. Special year-long residential (live-away) public schools for scientifically and mathematically talented students are one example of a program for the gifted and talented; high school programs that facilitate study at local and distant universities via computers and other electronic means are another example.

Finally, we have a term invented in the 1980s, namely the *at-risk learner*. At-risk learners are students whose poor academic achievement (typically in reading and math) flag them as students who are likely to become dropouts. Federal and state dollars support at-risk programs, and increasingly we find special tutorial programs for such learners beginning as early as the first grade (Pinnell et al., 1990). Although the term *at risk* did not exist in the 1960s, the Head Start program, which provided preschoolers with nutritional and academic support, was and still is a program designed to support at-risk learners.

Clearly one of the greatest challenges that you will experience as a teacher will stem from your attempt to sensitively and wisely respond to the diversity of sociocultural backgrounds and instructional needs among your students. As indicated earlier, your ability to respond appropriately to this challenge will be strongly influenced by your knowledge base and attitude regarding diversity. Traditionally, when considering a career in teaching, prospective teachers—particularly those oriented toward elementary teaching—have been asked to consider whether or not they really like children. An equally valid question for today's prospective teacher is: Will you welcome and value diversity in your classroom? At this point in your professional development this broad question will not be easy to answer, but you can gain some insight into your feelings about diversity by completing the Core Activity and other activities that follow.

Please note that the Core Activity specifies a certain type of classroom for observation. In some areas of the United States, such integrated classrooms will be difficult to locate. Our fundamental objective is to have prospective teachers observe teachers who respond to diversity in an exemplary manner. The degree of specific ethnic diversity is less important than the expertise manifested by the teacher. Also, we appreciate that some teacher education programs operate almost totally in environments that are rich in diversity. Hopefully, in such areas, the activities that follow will reinforce and extend the normal pattern of prestudent-teaching observation.

Finally, beyond the following activities, you can take two steps that will help you develop the multicultural knowledge base and pluralistic attitude alluded to earlier. Step 1 is to seek out information regarding professional organizations that are committed to clarifying and advancing the multicultural education agenda. Currently, the preeminent organization is the National Association for Multicultural Education (NAME). This organization, which came into existence in 1991, began to develop statewide chapters in 1996 so that members could participate in state and national meetings and projects. The organization publishes *Proceedings* from its annual meetings and a quarterly magazine entitled *Multicultural Education*. Membership dues for NAME in 1996 were $75 per year, and this included a subscription to *Multicultural Education*. For specific membership information contact Donna Gollnick by phone at (202) 416-6157 or by E-mail at "donna@ncate.org" or by mail at NCATE, 2029 K Street N.W., Suite 500, Washington, D.C. 20006.

Step 2 is to subscribe to a listserv concerned with multicultural education. One listserv worthy of your attention, MULTC-ED, provides an electronic forum for members and nonmembers of NAME. To join this listserv via E-mail, send a message to listserv@umdd.umd.edu and type in:

SUBSCRIBE MULTC-ED   <u> Groucho </u>   <u> Marx </u>
                                 Your First Name   Your Last Name

The list coordinators, Jack Levy (jlevy@gmu.edu) and Ruth Heidelback (rh19@umail.umd.edu), will send you specific information about how to send messages to all list members, to unsubscribe, and so on. Another valuable listserv, EDEQUITY, is sponsored by the Center for Equity and Diversity, Education Development Center, Inc., Chapel Street, Newton, MA 02158-1060. This listserv, according to its creators, is designed to encourage discussion between teachers and other practitioners, equity advocates, parents, counselors, and interested others. To subscribe, (a) send an E-mail message to the address "majordomo@confer.edc.org," (b) leave the subject line empty, and (c) in the body of the message, type in the following two words: subscribe edequity. Upon receiving your message, the administrator of this listserv will send you specific information about posting messages to listserv members, unsubscribing, and so forth.

Core Activity
OBSERVING DIVERSITY IN THE CLASSROOM

Observe for a full day or two half days in an upper (fourth, fifth, or sixth grade, junior high, or high school) classroom that has a rich diversity of ethnic and racial groups represented (approximately 50 percent nonwhite, if possible) as well as several students who are limited English proficient or who have learning disabilities of some kind. The teacher you observe should be identified as a successful teacher by your professor, and if possible the classroom should be in a school considered to be lower SES (socioeconomic status) in the school district. After your observation, do the following:

1. Answer these questions:
   (a) How would you feel if you were assigned to teach as a student teacher (or teacher) in this classroom?
   (b) Would you want to teach in this classroom? In this school? Why or why not?
2. Conduct an informal, semistructured interview with the teacher and/or the principal of the school. Try to discuss how the teacher and/or principal:
   (a) thinks and feels about the classroom diversity that he or she encounters
   (b) defines *multicultural education* and *multicultural instruction*

   Write a few paragraphs that compare and contrast your interviewee's perceptions of classroom diversity and multicultural education with those presented in this chapter. Where possible, share your findings with other prospective teachers.

Suggested Activity 1
OBSERVING MULTICULTURAL SETTINGS

Observe for a full day or two half days in a classroom that mirrors the following characteristics as closely as possible:

1. Predominantly middle-class students
2. 20 to 75 percent visibly ethnic students (African American, Hispanic American, Native American, or Asian American)
3. Several students who are mainstreamed
4. The school in which you observe should be considered a predominantly middle-class school by the principal.

   After the day's observation complete the following activities:

1. Answer these questions:
   (a) Did the teaching, learning, and classroom interaction in this classroom differ from that of the classroom you observed in your Core Activity? Did it differ from other classrooms that you have observed in?
   (b) How would you feel if you were assigned to teach as a student teacher or first-year teacher in this classroom? Would you want to teach in this classroom? School? Why? Why not?
2. Conduct an informal, semistructured interview with the teacher and/or the principal of the school. Try to discover how the teacher and/or principal:
   (a) feels about the level of classroom or school diversity with which he or she works
   (b) handles policies associated with mainstreaming or inclusion
   (c) orients teaching and evaluation toward a better match with students' special learning styles
   (d) views and defines *multicultural education*

Holt, Rinehart and Winston

Write a few paragraphs that compare and contrast your interviewee's perceptions of multicultural education with those presented in this chapter. Does your interviewee make a connection between multicultural education and special education (the education that mainstreamed and other "exceptional" children receive)? Where possible, share your findings with other prospective teachers.

Suggested Activity 2

OBSERVING THE SPECIAL NEEDS CLASSROOM

Most elementary, junior high, and high schools have special rooms and special teachers who work individually or in small groups with students who require special instruction for some reason. Typically, the teachers who provide this instruction have received special training to prepare them for this role, which includes providing support for the regular classroom teachers in the school. For the purpose of learning how to deal with diversity in the classroom, these resource room or special educators can be a valuable resource for prospective teachers. To tap into this resource perform the following:

1. Observe in a resource room for an entire morning, making special note of the physical differences between the resource classroom and the regular classroom. In the way of resources, what does the resource room have that the regular classroom doesn't? In addition, observe and take notes on the way that the resource room teacher interacts with his or her students. Please note that in your region or state, the resource room may have a different name. Seek out the room where individualized instruction for mainstreamed students with special learning needs is provided.

2. If possible, observe for an entire morning in a classroom where the resource room teacher helps the regular classroom teacher in the latter's classroom. This will occasionally occur when a severely challenged learner is placed into the mainstream classroom.

3. Conduct an informal, semistructured interview with the resource room teacher. Try to discover:

   (a) If the resource room teacher makes use of learning-style data or any other type of special information in designing effective instruction for his or her students

   (b) What the resource room teacher believes that the regular classroom teacher can do in her own classroom to create supportive, enabling learning environments for diverse learners

   (c) If the resource room teacher believes that there are specific teaching strategies or approaches to teaching that would benefit most of the children she teaches

   (d) If the school district has any special projects that involve mainstreaming students with severe disabilities, and if so, what the resource room teacher thinks about these projects

4. Write a few paragraphs that summarize what you have learned about creating supportive, enabling learning environments for students with special learning needs. Where possible, share your findings with other prospective teachers.

Suggested Activity 3

OBSERVING LEARNING/TEACHING STYLES

It is widely assumed that teachers who are adept at creating supportive, enabling learning environments for diverse students are able to do so because they have developed a flexible teaching style. They have developed an ability and commitment to the diverse learning styles and needs of their students. Sometimes the ability to flex begins with a heightened awareness of one's own learning style. Completion of the following worksheet, followed up by class or small-group discussions, should be an illuminating exercise.

The learning and teaching style analysis worksheet has been used in a variety of teacher education courses (Davidman, 1984). The worksheet is filled out after several conceptions of learning style are discussed. The learning style conceptions of James Renzulli, Linda Smith, Rita Dunn, and Gary Price, although different, have served as useful stimuli for teachers' self-analysis of their own learning styles. Renzulli and Smith define *learning style* in terms of the teaching strategies that students prefer to learn by. The strategies presented in their instrument are:

projects	independent study
drill and recitation	programmed instruction
peer teaching	lecture
discussion	simulation
teaching games	

The Dunn/Price conception and instrument, on the other hand, incorporate a wide range of variables that affect the way learners concentrate on, absorb, and retain new or difficult information and skills. The variables, which are listed next, are environmental, sociological, physical, and psychological in nature. The wide-ranging Dunn/Price conception is valuable because it reminds us that for some learners an environmental variable like light or warmth may be as critical to learning success as is a teaching strategy. The Dunn/Price variables are:

prefers learning through several ways	light
auditory preferences	warmth
visual preferences	formal design
tactile preferences	motivated/unmotivated
kinesthetic preferences	adult motivated
requires intake	teacher motivated
functions best in morning	persistent
functions best in late morning	responsible
functions best in afternoon	structure
functions best in evening	prefers learning alone
needs mobility	peer-oriented learner
sound	learning with adults

Holt, Rinehart and Winston

INSTRUCTIONS

Before you fill in the following worksheet, try to identify some of the best and worst learning experiences that you've had in the past five or so years. Then as you complete these sentences use these learning experiences as a source of data. In addition, for items 1 through 3, think about school and home learning environments, paying particular attention to the teachers' strategies, structure of the class, and any cognitive, affective, or environmental variables that you consider pertinent. Please refer to the preceding Dunn/Price and Renzulli/Smith lists as you complete this form. Complete items 7 and 8 only if you have had teaching experience.

Student Name: _____ Date: _____

WORKSHEET

1. I learn new and/or difficult information best when:

   (a) _____

   (b) _____

   (c) _____

   (d) _____

   (e) _____

   (f) _____

   (g) _____

2. I have trouble learning new and/or difficult information when:

   (a) _____

   (b) _____

   (c) _____

   (d) _____

   (e) _____

   (f) _____

   (g) _____

3. I find it *very* helpful to my learning if the learning environment is, or has:

   (a) _____

   (b) _____

   (c) _____

   (d) _____

   (e) _____

   (f) _____

   (g) _____

Student Name: _____   Date: _____

4. When I study, whether at home or at school, I like to:

    (a) _____

    (b) _____

    (c) _____

    (d) _____

    (e) _____

    (f) _____

5. The way that I learn is probably like that of others in many ways, but I think that it may be special because I:

    (a) _____

    (b) _____

    (c) _____

6. Between elementary school and today, my learning style preferences/needs have:
    ❑ Remained pretty much the same
    ❑ Changed moderately (please describe the changes below)
    ❑ Changed a great deal (please describe the changes below)

    _____

    _____

    _____

    _____

    _____

    _____

    _____

    _____

Student Name: _____   Date: _____

7. Regarding my teaching style, I will likely make good use of the following teaching strategies (or would if the resources were available). Put an *X* into the boxes in front of the appropriate strategies, and please fill in your own strategies if they are not here.

❏ Discussion
❏ Lecture (or minilectures)
❏ Drill and recitation
❏ Computer-assisted instruction
❏ Independent study
❏ Simulations
❏ Directed reading
❏ Learning centers

❏ Programmed instruction
❏ Games
❏ Project approach
❏ Peer tutoring
❏ Direct instruction
❏ Discovery learning
❏ Listening posts

Holt, Rinehart and Winston

Student Name: _____ Date :_____

8. Regarding a possible connection between my current learning style and my current teaching style, at this point I:
   ❏ See no connection
   ❏ See one or more possible connections (please describe below)

_____

_____

_____

_____

_____

_____

_____

_____

_____

_____

_____

_____

_____

_____

_____

_____

_____

_____

_____

_____

_____

_____

_____

Suggested Activity 4

OBSERVING SHELTERED ENGLISH INSTRUCTION

Although bilingual instruction (maintenance and transitional) is increasingly accepted as the most appropriate teaching strategy for second language learners, in some school settings it has proven difficult to provide enough teachers who are fluent in the learners' native tongue. For these learners, as well as for learners who are receiving dual language instruction, a special, and very sensible, approach to teaching the new language (English) has evolved. The approach is called *sheltered English instruction* or *specially designed academic instruction in English,* and the basic idea is to use a variety of strategies to make oral communication in core academic subjects such as science, math, and social studies as comprehensible as possible. For example, teachers using this approach usually simplify their oral input by using shorter sentences, speaking at a slower rate, and avoiding ambiguous vocabulary and idioms such as "Don't use off-the-wall ideas!" In addition, comprehension-minded teachers make greater use of visual aids, hand gestures, physical props, and manipulatives. General knowledge of second language acquisition also comes into play as sheltered English instructors positively react to the learners' silent period, as well as to their attempts to maintain the use of their native language. There is much more to sheltered English instruction, and it is our hope that the following observation task will stimulate your growth in this important area.

The Observation Task

With the help of your instructor identify several classrooms where sheltered English instruction is employed. Observe several lessons if possible.

1. If possible, observe in a class where the students speak three or more native languages and are in their first year of learning English. Typically, this teacher will not be fluent in any of the native languages spoken by the students.
2. As a contrast, attempt to observe a bilingual teacher working with the students at various levels of English proficiency. If time permits, interview both teachers regarding their use of sheltered English instruction techniques.

Holt, Rinehart and Winston

SHELTERED ENGLISH OBSERVATION FORM

Name: _____ Teacher: _____

Date: _____ Grade/Subject: _____

School: _____

Data Collection

1. Specifically, what did the teacher do to make his or her oral remarks comprehensible to the limited English proficient (LEP) learners in his or her class?*

   _____

   _____

   _____

   _____

2. How did his or her oral and nonverbal communication differ from communication that you have observed in other classrooms?

   _____

   _____

   _____

   _____

3. Did this teacher use cooperative learning groups or partners to increase student comprehension of instructions and lesson content? If "yes," how did the groups or partners appear to be functioning?

   _____

   _____

   _____

   _____

4. What, if anything, did you notice about the teacher's use of visual aids, manipulatives, or special props?

   _____

   _____

   _____

   _____

---

*Please note that in certain states, like California, the acronym LEP has been replaced by ELL, which stands for English language learner.

5. Beyond the variables mentioned earlier, what else did the teacher do to increase the students'comprehension of the lesson content?

_____

_____

_____

_____

6. How would you describe the reaction of the LEP learners to this instructional approach?

_____

_____

_____

_____

_____

Comparison, Contrast, and Analysis

1. Based on your observation(s) and possible interview(s), how would you describe the differences between sheltered English instruction and other approaches to effective instruction with which you are familiar? How would you describe the commonalities?

   _____

   _____

   _____

   _____

   _____

   _____

2. What were the significant differences between this classroom and other classrooms you have recently observed?

   _____

   _____

   _____

   _____

   _____

3. What did you like about the teaching you observed? What, if anything appeared dubious to you? What questions do you have about sheltered English instruction?

   _____

   _____

   _____

   _____

   _____

Student Name: _____   Date:_____

Journal Entry

Because this chapter focused on accepting and embracing the challenge of diversity and individual differences, your Journal Entry should concentrate on what you have learned about:

1. Yourself and your own potential to work with diverse student populations
2. Your desire to modify your teaching to meet individual student's needs
3. Your own thoughts and feelings about multicultural education, special education, bilingual education, and other types of supportive learning environments
4. Your own learning and (potential) teaching styles

_____

_____

_____

_____

_____

_____

_____

_____

_____

_____

_____

_____

_____

_____

_____

_____

_____

_____

_____

_____

Questions for Discussion

1. The authors assert that commitment to diversity, which implies a pervasive and consistent attention to individual differences, is a part of the tradition, symbolic rhetoric, and legislative framework of American education and is what makes the American classroom unique among the classrooms of the world.

   (a) Do you agree with these assertions? Why or why not?

   (b) If you don't totally agree with these assertions, to what extent do you believe that they are accurate?

2. What is the relationship between *special education* and *multicultural education*? Where do these terms overlap, diverge?

3. In discussing learning-style-informed education, some practitioners have charged that it is not practical. "You just can't custom tailor a learning environment for every learner in the class." What is your reaction to this assertion?

4. What are your thoughts about the following statement, which comments on the teaching style of a "multicultural" educator?

   By definition a multicultural educator's teaching style should be strongly influenced by the learning styles and learning needs of her students. She may enjoy teaching and learning in highly individualistic, competitive learning environments, love to lecture, and know and care very little about the history and demography of Mexico. But, if research or teacher experience has demonstrated that cooperative learning groups, high degrees of active student participation and discussion, and teacher knowledge of Mexican history have proven to be beneficial to the learning of her students, the multicultural educator will modify her teaching style to move in the direction of her students' learning styles and needs.

5. This chapter implies that a supportive/enabling classroom teacher will, among other things, strive to countervail and diminish the effects of racism, sexism, elitism, handicapism, and religious intolerance in our society by positively responding to diversity and individual differences in his instruction.

   (a) Do you think that this is an appropriate and realistic task for classroom teachers? Why? Why not?

   (b) As a future educator, how would you describe your own feelings about the various -*isms* just mentioned? Do these words, for example, represent forces that contemporary educators should be very knowledgeable about, or are they divisive topics worthy of minimal attention in an education program?

References

Banks, J. (1981). *Multiethnic education: Theory and practice* (p. 32). Boston: Allyn and Bacon.

Davidman, L. (1984). *Learning style and teaching style analysis in the teacher education curriculum: A synthesis approach.* (ERIC Document Reproduction Service No. ED 249183).

Davidman, L., and Davidman, P. (1997). *Teaching with a multicultural perspective: A practical guide* (2nd ed.). White Plains, N.Y.: Longman.

Eisner, E. W. (1991). What really counts in schools. *Educational Leadership* 48 (5).

Gay, G. (1983). Multiethnic education: Historical development and future prospects. *Phi Delta Kappan* 65 (8).

Gay, G. (1983). Ethnic minorities and educational equality. In *Multicultural education: Issues and perspectives* (2nd ed.), edited by J. A. Banks and C. A. Banks. Boston: Allyn and Bacon.

Grant, C. A., ed. (1977). *Multicultural education: Commitments, issues, and applications* (p. 2). Washington, D.C.: The Association for Supervision and Curriculum Development.

Jones, C. (May 18, 1992). Social services at school aids, inspires parents and students. *Los Angeles Times*, B1, B3.

Karasoff, P. (1991). Patricia Karasoff, the editor of *Strategies*, a bulletin that reports on the integration of students with severe disabilities, was reached at (415) 338-1162. The bulletin is published by the California Research Institute, 14 Tapia Drive, San Francisco, CA 94132. Call (415) 338-7847 for information about back issues.

Kozol, J. (1991). *Savage inequalities*. New York: Crown (division of Random House).

News and Issues. (1995). Number of poor children under six increased from 5 to 6 million 1987-1992. *News and Issues* 5 (1): 1-2. (*News and Issues* is a newsletter published by the National Center for Children in Poverty, which is part of the Columbia University School of Public Health, located at 154 Haven Avenue, New York, NY 10032 [212-927-8793].)

Nieto, S. (1992). *Affirming diversity: The sociopolitical context of multicultural education*. White Plains, N.Y.: Longman.

Pinnell, G. S., Fried, M. D., and Estice, R. M. (1990). Reading recovery: Learning how to make a difference. *The Reading Teacher* 43 (4): 282-295.

Sirotnick, K. (1990). Equal access to quality in public schooling: Issues in the assessment of equality and excellence. In *Access to knowledge: An agenda for our nation's schools*, edited by J. I. Goodlad and P. Keating. New York: The College Board.

Tetreault, M. (1993). Classrooms for diversity: Rethinking curriculum and pedagogy. In *Multicultural education: Issues and perspectives* (2nd ed.), edited by J. A. Banks and C. A. Banks. Boston: Allyn and Bacon.

GENERAL MULTICULTURAL EDUCATION RESOURCES

Banks, J. (1997). *Teaching strategies for ethnic studies* (6th ed.). Boston: Allyn and Bacon.

Banks, J., and Banks, C. A. (1995). *Handbook of research on multicultural education*. Indianapolis, Ind.: Macmillan.

Gollnick, D. M., and Chinn, P. C. (1994). *Multicultural education in a pluralistic society* (4th ed.). Columbus, Ohio: Merrill.

Hernandez, H. (1997). *Teaching in multilingual classrooms: A teacher's guide to context, process, and content*. Columbus, Ohio: Merrill.

Lessow-Hurley, J. (1990). *Foundations of dual language instruction*. White Plains, N.Y.: Longman.

Nieto, S. (1991). *Affirming diversity: The sociopolitical context of multicultural education*. White Plains, N.Y.: Longman.

Ramsey, P. G., Vold, E. B., and Williams, L. R. (1989). *Multicultural education: A source book*. New York: Garland.

Chapter 11

ON BECOMING A TEACHER

And, so, we will end with *you.* This book has been designed to be a travel book, intended to take you on a journey. Instead of purchasing an airline ticket or signing up for a cruise, you took a course, a course designed to introduce you to education and the world of schools. Of course, our readers are not strangers to school, in fact most have spent a large portion of their lives in one classroom or another. However, this journey was a "backstage tour," an opportunity for you to see students and schools from the other side of the footlights—if you will, through the eyes of the teachers.

You have been the reporter, the observer, the stranger in a not-so-strange land. You have looked at familiar objects through new lenses. You have recorded classroom behavior and tried in various ways to capture and thus better understand what goes on in schools. You have questioned children and adults about their experiences. You have seen yourself—three or thirteen years earlier—in some of those students. Old memories have been evoked by the smell of the school cafeteria and the empty gymnasium. The purpose of this journey, this backstage trip through school, has not been to simply gather facts, to learn how to use observational instruments, or to learn a few perspectives on education. Nor has it been a mere sentimental journey.

Henry David Thoreau, one of our most distinguished essayists and a very crusty observer of life, once said of travel, "It is not worthwhile to go around the world to count the cats in Zanzibar." In other words, travel can be a potent type of educational experience; it should do something to us and for us. We should be changed as a result of the travel, seeing ourselves and our world differently as a result of observing life in Zanzibar or in P.S. 22. We will have wasted our time and money if we just collected facts or worse, if we passively experienced the journey, like a film that we really weren't interested in seeing or discussing. The purpose of this chapter, then, is to help you think about your journey, putting what you have learned into perspective.

Having given you information and insights into classrooms and the people who inhabit them, we turn now to a different focus. Socrates once proclaimed that the aim of education is to "know thyself." How has your work in this course deepened your understanding of yourself? Has it clarified your understanding of what is involved in teaching? Has it given you a richer sense of what is involved? Has it helped you to answer the questions, "Is teaching for you?" and "Are you for teaching?" Some of you may already have solid answers to these questions, but most of you, we suspect, will benefit from one final set of thought-provoking observation

211

and analysis activities as you attempt to develop clearer answers to these questions. Now, as your journey in this course is nearing completion, you will become the object of observation and analysis. And the observation activities that follow, like many others in this text, will involve you with tools that will prove valuable to you in journeys that reach far beyond this course. These self-observation/analysis activities will lead you into a personal goal/objective-setting effort that we hope will be the beginning of your career as an active, analytical, self-directed professional.

Core Activity
MAKING YOURSELF A TEACHER

The great majority of people who teach children go through a carefully sequenced program of academic and professional courses. They are said to "have gone through" teacher education. They have been "prepared." In one sense, this is correct. But in another, it is misleading. To "go through" teacher education and to "be prepared" are much too passive for what ought to happen.

Becoming a good teacher, like becoming a good musician or a good athlete, requires a good deal of self-initiative and self-direction. Training helps. Courses are important. Ultimately, however, the teacher makes himself or herself a good teacher. In effect, the individual is both the maker and the made, both the artist and the work of art. Such a point of view requires the maker—the future teacher—to have both the will to make the changes and the idea of what he or she is making. By "will" we mean the desire and persistence to work toward the goal of becoming a skilled and dedicated teacher. By "idea" we mean a clear vision of what is being made, a blueprint that guides your activity. For instance, if a prospective teacher discovers that he is shy, he needs to overcome this condition. He needs to put himself into situations where he is forced to reach out to others and begin to be comfortable in what is the rather public role of the teacher. Or, if a prospective teacher is a big talker, but a poor listener, she needs to learn how to limit her talking, ask more questions, and carefully and patiently listen to what others are saying.

It is our intention to assist you in developing some of the ideas that should guide your own efforts to make yourself a teacher. In order to do this we urge you to complete three final steps.

First, review all of your answers to the exercises in this chapter with an eye toward identifying areas of strength and areas needing your attention. (If you have not completed all of the exercises, complete them before going any further.)

Second, after you have done the review, list your strengths and areas needing your attention in very specific terms. This is an important step, and you need to take time and give your full attention to it.

AREAS OF STRENGTH

1. _____

2. _____

3. _____

4. _____

Holt, Rinehart and Winston

5. _____

6. _____

7. _____

8. _____

9. _____

10. _____

11. _____

12. _____

AREAS NEEDING ATTENTION

1. _____

2. _____

3. _____

4. _____

5. _____

6. _____

7. _____

8. _____

9. _____

10. _____

11. _____

12. _____

Third, and finally, you need to develop some specific goals. Because none of us will ever be "the perfect teacher" and because we will always need to find ways to improve, we are not suggesting that you identify everything needed to reach such an unreachable goal. Rather, we want you to state in quite specific terms what you believe are five objectives that will bring you closer to becoming a good teacher. These five objectives should be based on what you have done earlier; they should be realistic, practical, and attainable objectives. For instance, "Making myself a great math teacher" is much too general. So, too, is "Getting over being shy." A more appropriate objective might be, "I will learn to maintain eye contact with people while speaking to them." Or, "I will learn to listen carefully to what people are saying to me."

Objective 1: _____

_____

Objective 2: _____

_____

Objective 3: _____

_____

Objective 4: _____

_____

Objective 5: _____

_____

The important point is that these are *your* objectives and that you use them to guide your efforts at making yourself the best teacher that you are capable of becoming.

Suggested Activity 1

KNOWING THYSELF

Winston Churchill, who arguably was the greatest statesman of the twentieth century, once described Russia as an enigma wrapped in a mystery. So, too, is the self, but few of us recognize this. If we reflect upon who we are for a moment, we can come up with words or ideas that describe or explain who we are. But this description/explanation is probably a very superficial view of ourselves. Would our parents come up with the same description? Would our best friend or roommate see us the same way? Would a psychologist probing our unconscious simply confirm our own list of words and ideas?

One way to look at self, to approximate who we are, is to think of certain dimensions of self. This approach has been conceptualized in the Johari Window. In it, the self is divided into four panes of a window.

The first pane is called the *Arena* and represents that part of self that is known to both ourselves and to others. It is that part of the self that we present to the public, that we recognize, and of which we take ownership. This is familiar territory.

The second pane (moving down) is the *Private Self*. Here is the self that we typically keep secret but that we might under special circumstances share with someone close to us. Often our fears and insecurities, our doubts and secret ambitions and passions are hidden here.

Self

| Things I Know | Things I Don't Know |

Things They Know	
Arena	Blind Spot
Others Things They Don't Know	
Private Self	Mystery

The third pane (upper right) is called the *Blind Spot*. This is the self that others see but that we don't see. Contained here is a self that, if revealed to us, would surprise us. Sometimes the Blind Spot contains pleasant characteristics and sometimes unpleasant characteristics. It is not unlike a person with a sign pinned to the back of his/her coat.

The fourth pane is called the *Mystery*. Here is the self that neither we nor outside observers are aware of. It is completely hidden from view, but it may be a very strong force in our lives. It may contain dreams and passions and fantasies of which we are not consciously aware. It is our mystery, and although we may come to know more and more of it, the mystery will never disappear (Luft, 1970).

During the next few days, complete your own Johari Window. To do this, follow these steps:

First, list five adjectives or phrases you would use to describe yourself accurately to others.

1. _____

2. _____

3. _____

4. _____

5. _____

Second, list five adjectives or phrases that you feel someone else who knows you well would use to describe you.

1. _____

2. _____

3. _____

4. _____

5. _____

Third, choose a roommate or classmate who, you believe, knows you well and ask that person to thoughtfully list five adjectives or phrases that describe you.

1. _____

2. _____

3. _____

4. _____

5. _____

Fourth, compare the lists. What have these three angles of viewing revealed? What are the similarities in the lists? What are the differences? How do you explain the differences? Think about what you have learned about yourself from the exercise so far.

Fifth, your instructor may or may not choose to put you into small groups to go over what you have learned in the first four steps. At this point, however, you should fill in as fully as you can your own Johari Window.

Holt, Rinehart and Winston

QUESTIONS

1. What happened in this exercise that confirmed your own view of yourself? (What was not a surprise?)
2. What surprised you about yourself?
3. Has your Mystery window pane become smaller or larger? How? Why?

_____

_____

_____

_____

_____

_____

_____

_____

_____

_____

_____

_____

_____

_____

_____

_____

_____

_____

_____

_____

_____

Suggested Activity 2
YOUR PERSONAL PROS AND CONS FOR TEACHING

The next step in our set of self-observation activities will give you the chance, first, to compare your reasons for going into teaching with a list of reasons that in-service teachers have identified and, second, to examine and comment on a set of reasons that explains why some people do not go into teaching or end their career rather quickly.

DIRECTIONS

1. First read each list carefully. Then, on the first column rate the reasons in list 1 from 1 through 6 that together explain why you are going into teaching. Give the strongest reason a rating of 1, the next-strongest a rating of 2, and so on. Then, do the same with list 2, but this time rate only the reasons that have meaning to you. Give the strongest reason a rating of 1 and so on.

LIST 1 (THE REASONS WHY PEOPLE ENTER TEACHING)

_____ Enjoy working with students

_____ Good fringe benefits (e.g., health insurance, long vacations, etc.)

_____ Doing important and honorable work

_____ Geographic flexibility

_____ Chance to work with people who share my goals

_____ Preferable to options in the business world

_____ Job stability

_____ Doing something good for the community

_____ Daily/yearly schedule that gives me time to myself

_____ Pleasant surroundings and working conditions

LIST 2 (THE REASONS WHY PEOPLE DO NOT GO INTO TEACHING OR LEAVE EARLY)

_____ Personally did not enjoy school and do not want to be part of it

_____ Looking for more material rewards from work than can be gained from teaching

_____ Do not want to be a disciplinarian

_____ As a teacher, not enough influence in educational issues and conditions of work

_____ As a teacher, not enough opportunities for personal growth

_____ Too much "out-of-school work" (e.g., preparations and paper corrections)

2. What does your set of ratings tell you about your reasons for going into teaching? Did your ratings in any way surprise you? If so, please explain why.

_____

_____

_____

_____

_____

_____

_____

_____

3. Read the second list of reasons and comment on how you think these factors may or may not influence your decision to begin and maintain a career in teaching. Explain why these particular reasons are meaningful or not meaningful to you.

_____

_____

_____

_____

_____

Holt, Rinehart and Winston

Suggested Activity 3
YOUR IDEAL SCHOOL

As a result of years of schooling, and more recently as a result of your field observations, you have developed a set of standards about schools. In fact, you have an ideal school in your mind. Much of what you think about yourself and education is wrapped up in that ideal. The following questions will help you learn about and identify factors of your ideal school. By responding to each of the questions, you will reveal dimensions of your ideal *and* of yourself.

1. What is the setting for your ideal school? Rural? Suburban? Inner city? In what part of the country or state? Be as explicit as possible.

2. What is the grade level of this school? What are the students like?

3. What is your classroom like? Physically (draw it if that helps)? Psychologically?

4. Describe the building (age, design, furnishings, outstanding features).

5. What other adults (if any) are part of your classroom?

6. What kind of relationships exists among the faculty members? Between you and your supervisor? How much supervision do you want?

7. What are some of the things you want to have happen in your ideal school?

8. What do your answers reveal about you and your career aspirations?

Holt, Rinehart and Winston

Suggested Activity 4
SETTING PERFORMANCE PRIORITIES

"The good teacher" is a practical idea, but it is also an ideal. As elementary and secondary school students, we trudged off to school each September, hoping that this year would be different, that this year we would get "the good teacher," the one who would like us and teach us to like school. Sometimes we came close to the ideal, but usually not.

There is, of course, no ideal teacher. Nor is there one set of characteristics or competencies that are ideal for all teaching situations. However, there has been a substantial amount of exhortation, debate, and research in this area in recent years. The competency- or performance-based movement in teacher education, which gained momentum during the 1970s, is a result of all this ferment, and it has produced several useful lists of important teacher competencies. For example, as a result of an extensive study at Iowa State University, Dick Mannette (1984) and his associates came up with a thorough list of teacher competencies. These competencies, or performance areas, are based on teaching effectiveness research as well as on the practical desires of principals, school boards, and superintendents.

These competencies—or criteria, as they are called in Mannette's assessment instrument—were distributed into four major performance categories: productive teaching techniques, classroom management, positive interpersonal relations, and professional responsibilities. You will recognize many of the performance areas, or competencies, listed next as the "basic stuff" of teaching, and it is almost certain that you will be evaluated in terms of *some* of these criteria if you choose to become a teacher. Therefore, it will be useful now to consider a plan for personal growth in teaching. Read through the list that follows and (a) put a check (√) next to those performance areas in which you believe you currently possess some skill or strength and (b) put a plus sign (+) next to those areas in which you believe you have a lot to learn (high-growth areas).*

In some of the performance areas, particularly performance category 4, you may find it difficult to rate yourself. *You do not need to put a √ or a + next to each of the twenty-six performance areas to complete this activity.* Indeed, rating yourself in half of these performance areas will be a positive step toward completing the final and most important activity in this chapter.

---

*Please note that the list employed in this text is the author's revision of materials presented in the previously cited document co-authored by Richard Mannette.

Holt, Rinehart and Winston

Student Name: _____   Date: _____

| PERFORMANCE CATEGORY 1 (PRODUCTIVE TEACHING TECHNIQUES) | Strength Area | High-Growth Area |

The teacher is able to:

1. Demonstrate effective lesson-planning skills _____ _____

2. Demonstrate effective lesson-sequence and unit-planning skills _____ _____

3. Effectively implement lesson plans _____ _____

4. Motivate students _____ _____

5. Effectively communicate with students _____ _____

6. Effectively diagnose students _____ _____

7. Provide students with specific evaluative feedback _____ _____

8. Display a thorough knowledge of subject matter _____ _____

9. Set appropriate expectations for student achievement _____ _____

10. Provide learning opportunities for individual/ idiosyncratic learners _____ _____

11. Effectively manage classroom learning time _____ _____

12. Select and effectively teach content that is congruent with the prescribed curriculum _____ _____

Student Name: _____   Date: _____

PERFORMANCE CATEGORY 2 (CLASSROOM MANAGEMENT)	Strength Area	High-Growth Area
13. Make effective use of time, materials, and human resources	_____	_____
14. Demonstrate evidence of personal organization	_____	_____
15. Set appropriate standards for student behavior	_____	_____
16. Organize students for effective instruction	_____	_____

PERFORMANCE CATEGORY 3
(POSITIVE INTERPERSONAL RELATIONS)

	Strength Area	High-Growth Area
17. Demonstrate effective interpersonal relationships with others	_____	_____
18. Demonstrate awareness of the needs of students	_____	_____
19. Promote positive self-concept(s)	_____	_____
20. Demonstrate sensitivity in relating to students	_____	_____
21. Promote self-discipline and responsibility	_____	_____

PERFORMANCE CATEGORY 4
(PROFESSIONAL RESPONSIBILITIES)

	Strength Area	High-Growth Area
22. Demonstrate employee responsibilities	_____	_____
23. Support school regulations and policies	_____	_____
24. Assume responsibilities outside the classroom as they relate to school	_____	_____
25. Engage in professional self-evaluation	_____	_____
26. Respond positively to suggested improvements in a timely manner	_____	_____

Student Name: _____   Date:_____

Journal Entry

Because this is the final chapter in this workbook and because a major objective of this workbook was to place you into a position to make a more informed choice about entering, or not entering, the teaching profession, it would be appropriate in this final Journal Entry for you to:

1. Share your decision
2. Explain why you have made this decision
3. Discuss how the journey that this workbook led you through contributed to your decision or the reasons for your decision

_____

_____

_____

_____

_____

_____

_____

_____

_____

_____

_____

_____

_____

_____

_____

_____

_____

_____

_____

Questions for Discussion

1. Which two activities in this workbook were most illuminating for you? Why?

2. Which of your five specific objectives are you going to "work" on first?

3. How did the rating and self-analysis activities in this chapter lead you to specify objectives that were a surprise to you?

4. If you had been asked to produce a set of five "growth" objectives at the beginning of the course, which of the final five that you produced would likely not have been included?

References

Luft, J. (1970). *Group processes: An introduction to group dynamics* (2nd ed.). Palo Alto, Calif.: National Press.

Mannette, R., and Stow, S. B. (1984). *Clinical manual for teacher performance evaluation.* Ames, Iowa: Iowa State University Foundation.

INDEX